Minnie of the Maritimes

Tellwell Talent
www.tellwell.ca

ISBN
978-0-2288-0361-4 (Hardcover)
978-0-2288-0360-7 (Paperback)
978-0-2288-0362-1 (eBook)

Minnie of the Maritimes

JUDITH TAIT

For all the women of the Maritimes,
who loved this land.

PROLOGUE

Minnie could smell the warm earthy scent of crushed wild grasses as she carefully made her way along the narrow path toward the bunkhouse. Stepping into a smooth hollow, her step faltered, the bowl of hot biscuits and ham slices in her hands and the bag of cold root beer on her shoulder were making her balance awkward. Usually she wasn't allowed to go anywhere near the working men, but her mother was in the middle of putting up the first strawberries and her sister was a better help in the kitchen. It was too hot in there anyway and she welcomed the sweet meadow's breeze as it dried the moisture on her face.

The men hired to look after the orchards were usually very polite and took their caps off when her mother brought their lunches out. Mostly too grizzled and shabby for a second glance, some new faces, younger men from away, replaced a couple of experienced men who didn't show up this season. Minnie saw them stub-out their cigarettes as they rose to greet her, shyly removing their caps, as in a chorus line. One of the new men stepped forward to take the bowl from her hands before she had a chance to set it down, brushing her fingers briefly and giving her a wide smile. She ducked her chin to hide her quick gasp, passing the clinking bag of bottles to one of the older men, her fingers still tingling from the unexpected touch of a stranger. Her nose picked up the male scent of sharp sweat, and the wet dog smell of unwashed clothes.

That reminded her of the message to be delivered from her father.

"Wednesday is wash day this week," she whispered, "Mother says come to the kitchen to fetch hot water, don't forget."

The old man who had taken a root beer and opened it up on a metal ring attached to the door looked up in surprise.

"Isn't it Saturday, usually, Miss?"

"Yes, but Father wants to go to town this Saturday and says whoever needs to go, can go with him then. You'll need clean clothes, yes?" She said it with a smile, so it didn't sound like the order it was.

The men scrubbed their own clothes in an old metal tub, like the one they washed the dog in at home. A clothes line with wooden pegs sagged between the bunkhouse corner and an ancient Chinese elm nearby.

"Sort out who does what between yourselves," she said. She backed away, then waited as the same young man handed back the empty bowl.

"Thanks for the grub, Miss, and thank your mother; it's the best we get anywhere." That flash of white teeth again, as she turned away, blushing.

She held up her hand, palm forward, an impersonal goodbye. To the men watching her leave, swaying like the meadow flowers at her feet, it was a blessing from Mother Mary herself.

THE JOURNEY

IMAGE 1

One

The crack of ice under the wheel rims and the lurch of the buggy from the horses gait as they gamely stepped in tandem over the uneven ground distracted Minnie from the tension radiating from the man beside her. Passing her grandmother's yard she didn't turn her head, afraid she'd see a face behind a twitching lace curtain. She did look longingly at the small white church on the corner. It had been four months since attending her last service before she started to show. Hitting a pothole that bounced her off the hard wooden seat her father made a sound at the back of his throat that could have been an apology, of sorts. He'd remained silent through the emotional turmoil at home, but then he was always "a deep river," as his wife would say, usually with a sigh. He hadn't helped Minnie climb into the high seat of the buggy, preferring to put her trunk in the back at that moment, avoiding any contact.

Reaching the crossroad, they turned right, her father slapping the reins to urge the horses into a quicker pace. As they passed the tiny two roomed schoolhouse on the corner Minnie turned her head away to keep from asking who would be replacing her as the teacher. As one of the church elders her father would have been informed, unless it had not been passed on to him, being the parent of the disgraced teacher beside him now. Her family's reputation in the country community would never recover its previous station, but they would survive. It's not as if half the community didn't have skeletons in their own closets.

Minnie sighed again, burrowing deeper into her coat that was now straining across her belly. She should have left ages ago but mail to Montreal took weeks to make its way there and back with a reply from the Sisters. A good place recommended by her parish minister for girls from good families who find themselves in trouble. Minnie always thought of those words in italics or visualised them as if cross stitched like her first attempt at an embroidered sampler. She concentrated now on the steaming rumps of the horses as they strained to climb the last hill before reaching town.

It was a tiny village of three stores, a post office, a survey office which shared a desk with the local coroner, and a larger school for the townies (as the farm kids liked to call the local children). Her father nodded to several well-dressed couples, clicking his tongue to pick up the horses pace again to avoid any attempt at conversation. Swiftly going by the last piece of flat dyke land, and then bumping over the connecting drainage pit, Minnie could see the train station and platform ahead. Soon another life would begin. Not the one she had expected, with a farmer husband working the land beside her father, with her cooking and cleaning and attending church, as the women in her family had always done.

Not true she thought again.

Her ancestors left everything in Ireland to cross the sea to an unknowable future. They had worked hard and flourished. She had been a restless child, reading everything, although the books available were limited to old tomes in an attic trunk or passed out for church catechism prizes. Hardly enough to stimulate a mind as inquisitive as hers, but teaching the little ones had given her an outlet for her energy. It made the winters pass without just the numbing silence found at home.

Home. Would she return? Could she? A question not asked and an answer not offered. Her father pulled the reins hard right to get them in line with a few other traps, wagons and buggies beside the soot stained station. Once again Minnie found her way to the ground unassisted while her father busied himself carrying the trunk into the station. She remained by the horses, giving their noses a gentle touch with her gloved hand, then turned to see her father stepping out with her ticket. Glancing at her briefly he addressed the horses' tails with instructions meant for her: the address of the convent and the closest station to it in Montreal. He passed her an envelope and the ticket, barely touching her hand. Looking upward he spoke softly, "You are to go to your aunt's house in PEI after this is over. She has written to your mother. I'll send you the ticket when I hear how you fare."

His eyes closed for a moment, and then he turned and hugged her tightly.

"My girl, my girl, be safe. This will pass." It seemed like he was drawing in a breath to say more but suddenly reached for the reins. "The train arrives within the hour."

He touched the brim of his hat and Minnie stood back. She watched the slumped shoulders in the dark coat ride back to the main road, the buggy growing smaller until tears blurred her vision.

IMAGE 2

Two

A deep breath and a quick look around brought her back to reality. With a growing rumble and a screeching wheeze the train slowed and stopped at the station entrance. Minnie stepped over the station's doorsill and, seeing her trunk labelled and waiting in the corner, looked up to see an advancing porter. Checking for her ticket he asked if he could put her trunk on board. She nodded, hoping the few pennies she had saved by not attending church and putting them in the collection box would be enough for his help. He showed her where her seat was and where her trunk was stored, then smiled as she placed the pennies in his hand.

It was, she realised after sitting stiffly near the train's dusty window, an adventure. From now on she would hold her head up and go through the days ahead, one by one, with integrity and calm. That lasted until she had to pee again, as happened so often these days. Not willing to ask anyone if there were any facilities, she looked up and down the aisle until she saw a woman come out of a small door, while adjusting her hat. Minnie approached her, but before she could decide what to say, the woman held the door open for her with a smile. Blushing, Minnie entered her first indoor lavatory — an adventure, for sure, on a now rocking train.

Back in her seat, Minnie got another smile from the same woman who was opening a wicker basket and delivering a cloth wrapped package to the man beside her. He took it without looking up from his newspaper. Why hadn't she thought of bringing some food? Always hungry, she had been careful not to ask for seconds or appear like she was helping herself from the pantry at home. But someone, her sister perhaps, could have wrapped up a biscuit or some apples. It would take all day to get to Halifax where she changed trains, then overnight to Montreal.

Just then, the ticket master arrived to gather tickets. Behind him, the same porter who had carried her trunk pushed a tea service on a swaying cart. Looking at the pale, tense face of the young woman, he passed her a cup and saucer, a sandwich wrapped in butcher paper and a small cupcake in a foil twist. At her raised eyebrows, he pulled a tray out of her armrest and placed a paper napkin, a small pitcher of cream and a paper packet of sugar in front of her.

"We will be in Halifax at 6 PM," he said, pouring her some tea, "and you can buy your supper in a café there before your next connection."

He moved on with a smile. Minnie let go of her reticule and reached for the tea.

Before reaching Windsor, their first stop, the porter removed her tea items with a nod and Minnie settled in to watch the frozen countryside slide by. She wanted to read what was in her father's envelope but couldn't bring herself to open it in public; her emotions already too close to the surface. The motion of the train after leaving Windsor station lulled her into a light sleep.

Flickering images of a face, a small crooked smile, and the warmth that flooded her body at his touch jerked her awake, the thunder of blood pounding in her ears. Removing her coat and folding it carefully on her seat, she rolled her stiff shoulders and made her way back to the lavatory, once again under the gaze of the woman in the seat across the aisle.

On her return, the woman had moved into the seat beside her coat. Oh, no! Conversation was not what she wanted, but a sudden kick from the child made her instinctively place her hand briefly on her belly. The woman smiled, something she seemed to do often, and nodding at her sleeping husband said, "I hope you don't mind my sharing your seat. I am dreadfully bored."

Tilting her head toward Minnie she added softly, "Your first?"

Minnie nodded once, hoping the woman would take her hesitance for an obvious desire not to open a conversation.

"God has seen in his wisdom, not to give us children. I'd so wished..." the woman's voice trailed off and her eyes drifted to the passing view.

Minnie sat awkwardly, the kicks more pronounced with the child stirring in protest at her sitting for so long.

"So, are you stopping in Halifax?" the woman asked. "I'm sorry," she held out her ungloved hand, "I'm Mary Cobourn; that is my husband Edward." She smiled at the man still peacefully sleeping, his newspaper having slipped to the floor. "We live in Quebec, in Laval, actually. We've been visiting Edward's family in Yarmouth; such a long journey." She smoothed the lap of her dress, realizing she may have intruded into the young woman's privacy.

"I change trains in Halifax for Montreal," Minnie murmured, hoping she had avoided answering the woman's first question.

"Oh, such a wonderful city. Have you been there before? You must have family meeting you, yes?" Mary was curious and determined to have some decent conversation to while away the hours ahead. Minnie blushed, something she was never prone to do until recently.

"No, no family and this is my first visit," she mumbled.

"Ah," was Mary's knowing reply; once again glancing at her uncomfortable companion's averted face. "I see. Forgive me for being so forward, but," she paused, "the father?"

Growing redder, head bowed, Minnie shook her head.

"Humm, what will you do?"

The woman's persistence unnerved Minnie, and yet she'd had no one to confide in and it was so tempting. But, drawing in a breath, all she could reply was "I go to Prince Edward Island, to live, after..." she hesitated, "alone. I mean, I'll live with my aunt and her family."

"I see," said Mary, again.

Good heavens, thought Minnie, was she going to have to answer questions from strangers all the way to Montreal? She turned her head to the window and wished she could have brought a novel with her to shut out uninvited and deeply embarrassing questions like this. But truly the questions had been difficult only because of her circumstances, not because they were unusual. She had been held in such deep contempt at home she'd rarely spoken to anyone these last two months.

"I can't do this, I simply cannot do this!" she heard her mother say, her shrill voice rising through the vent in her room.

It was met by her father's low rumble, something about talking to the minister. Minnie lifted her eyes, grey and so troubled compared to the clear blue eyes of her fellow passenger.

"You are not the first my dear, and it is always the woman who pays the price." Mary sighed, then looking thoughtful, reached out and patted Minnie's hand. She stood, and glancing at her husband, said, "I hope we can chat more later, if you don't mind I mean."

What did it matter? thought Minnie. She would never see her again after parting ways, so she smiled a little and replied, "If you wish."

Later that day they did speak again, or rather Minnie answered Mary's questions about her home, her teaching and her church activities. When Mary tried tactfully to ask again about her "gentleman friend," Minnie shook her head; she had closed her mind to him and would not answer.

Three

Changing trains in Halifax was made simple once again by the cheerful porter who arrived by her side as she slipped on her coat and adjusted her hat. With her trunk placed on a dolly he guided her to the right platform, checked the label and pointed out a small café inside the station.

"You shouldn't leave your trunk unattended here," he shouted above the chaos of the busy platform. "Go find a table and I'll bring it along."

The café was warm, so Minnie draped her coat over a chair by the window and signaled the porter, placing the last of her pennies in his hand.

"Thank you for your kindness," she paused, "and for the tea."

"You are most welcome, Mam, have a safe journey." Touching his billed hat, he disappeared into the crowd.

Feeling alone in the crowded café, Minnie sat and opened the envelope, finding several pound notes and a letter. She smoothed the single page and read her father's shaky script.

"These funds were being kept for your trousseau," he wrote, "same as your sisters, but it will serve you better now. The days ahead will not be easy. We know and share your disappointment that things have not turned out the way we had wished for you. Your mother and I share the blame and feel we did not protect you well enough. We only pray to God in His mercy that the future will bring you the happiness you deserve and that this misfortune will fade from your memory with time. Your aunt Margaret in PEI is a good Christian woman and will treat you kindly. We send you there not as a punishment, but as a chance at a better future than you would face here. Send any replies in care of Rev. Moody; he will keep your confidence secure. As the good and responsible daughter you have been in the past, please follow our wishes. We mean only the best for you. Also, follow the Sister's orders. They will be strict but will provide what is needed. Your father, Mathew Healy."

Minnie sat still for a long time remembering family dinners and the busy life on the farm with a mixed emotion of love and regret. Her stomach rumbled and a glance at the wall clock got her up to order a simple supper using one of the pound notes. She would need small change for the rest of the journey.

She didn't think the next porter would give her a free tea and she was right. He was a rather large, surly man, whose clothes smelled of sweat and tobacco. He carried her trunk in his arms to her train's seat section and pushed it roughly under the bottom storage rack by the entrance. He held out his hand for her coins, turning away and looking for the next customer.

Before Minnie could mount the steps, she felt a soft touch on her sleeve. Startled, she turned to find the now familiar blue eyes of Mary Cobourn.

"You couldn't hear me calling over this racket, but I couldn't miss this opportunity to give you my address. Please," her voice was unsteady, "I've spoken to my husband about your situation." She glanced down the platform where he waited with their luggage, obviously impatient. "We have long considered adoption, but Edward was wary, not knowing the proper way of doing this. I mean, not knowing the baby's parents… it's all so awkward!" She held up her hand to let her husband know she would just be a moment longer. "Please," she said again, this time more firmly, "let me know where and when, and we will contact the convent and make sure the proper papers will be arranged. Will you consider this? I must hurry, we are in a different carriage this time, but I feel our meeting was not by chance." She pressed a card into Minnie's hand and gave her fingers a squeeze. "Good luck, my dear, and write to me!"

Minnie, speechless, could only nod and climb the steps as the train whistle blew.

She found a window seat, hoping no one would need the space beside her. Closing her eyes, she breathed in and out slowly, wanting to throw back her head and howl like the dog on the farm when there was a full moon.

"Steady girl, steady," her father's voice from her childhood whispered in her ear.

Tears leaked from under her eyelashes. Hastily wiping at them with her pocket hankie, she saw the last of the passengers make their way towards her. The train was filling up with townsfolk holding wrapped packages and excited children. Their chatter was noisy even over the chuffing of the now moving train. A couple with two small children, a girl and a boy, approached, taking the seat across the aisle. The mother looked over and in accented English asked if she could put the little girl in the seat beside

Minnie. Looking at the shy toddler with her thumb in her mouth, she nodded.

"Assez tu," the mother whispered, "Tu attende la, oui? Restez ici."

Reaching into her knitted bag, one of vast proportions, she handed a sock doll with a darned smiling face to her daughter then turned to settle the little boy beside his father.

"Je m'apple Minnie, comme s'apple tu elle?" Minnie's French was limited to phrases learned from the Acadians who worked on the farm during harvest time.

"Michelle," the child whispered, adding, "Rosette," holding up her doll.

The rest of the evening passed quickly. Minnie entertained the little girl with simple games until Michelle curled up on the seat and went to sleep with her thumb firmly in her mouth. Minnie stood up to stretch and nodded at the mother's grin.

"You'll be a good mother," she said, the round bump of Minnie's belly in her gaze.

"I was a teacher," Minnie said, praying for no more questions.

She found the train's lavatory by herself this time. It was larger than the last one but not nearly so clean, although it did have some soap and a dubious looking towel hung on a rack by the spotted sink.

Back in the aisle she pulled out her trunk far enough to open the lid and retrieve her shawl. Inside its folds was a small cloth-wrapped cake and a note in her sister's neat handwriting.

"God bless, love always, Mildred."

Closing the lid and pushing the trunk back in place, Minnie stood up, swaying with the train's motion. A wave of dizziness swept over her. Reaching for the nearest hard surface to steady herself, she felt a strong grip on her arm.

"Please, seat yourself Madame, you are very pale."

Minnie slid into the seat beside her, leaning her head back until her vision cleared. A young man no more than twenty years old knelt on one knee beside her.

"Take your time. Can I get you anything — a cup of tea, perhaps?"

The light reflecting on his glasses hid his eyes but his voice was kind. Minnie nodded, mainly so she could have a moment to gather her wits. She wanted to laugh and she wanted to cry; she did neither. About to stand and retreat to her own seat, the young man returned holding out a cup and saucer, dripping with tea.

"Sorry, I overfilled it with milk," he said, passing her the cup and awkwardly holding onto the saucer. "Sugar, I put sugar in as well, I hope that's alright."

Minnie took a large gulp of the tepid liquid then held out the cup while he poured in the remaining tea. She reached for the saucer and resting it on her hankie, said, "Thank you sir. I stood up too quickly that's all. No need to" ....she was going to say fuss, but that sounded rude, "worry," she finished.

He had the most wonderful brown eyes, although at the moment they were filled with concern.

"Can I help you to your seat? I mean there is no rush, you can stay here until my family returns from the dining car."

Minnie didn't even know there was a dining car. She stood up, handing back the cup and saucer.

"No, I'm fine now, really. You've been too kind. I share my seat with a toddler; I wouldn't want her to roll off while I'm not there."

That seemed to reassure the young man and gave him the intended impression that she was not alone. He tipped an imaginary hat and turned to go, then turned back to face her.

"Actually, we will be heading to the sleeping compartments after supper, so if you need to — I mean if your family doesn't have enough room — you can stretch out here." He hesitated. "At least until morning if you don't have a sleeping compartment, I mean."

Now he was blushing. Sweet boy, thought Minnie. "Thank you, I just might." This time she was smiling.

Carefully holding the cup and saucer, he slid back the metal door between the carriages and disappeared. Minnie made her way back to her seat, and noting the little family beside her was asleep, she settled by the rosy cheeked Michelle. Tucking her shawl over both of them, exhausted emotionally and physically, she quickly went to sleep, rocked by the swaying of the train and the clack of the wheels.

Four

She woke in the middle of the night to the train whistle's wailing and the brakes grinding screech as it slowed towards Truro station. Michelle responded with a matching wail. Her mother in the seat across the aisle leaned over and spoke softly to her in French. The child nodded and took her mother's hand as they made their way to the lavatory. Good idea, thought Minnie, stretching her aching back as the lights came up. Passengers gathered their packages and sleepy children, getting ready to depart.

How much longer to Montreal? The train seemed like it was a slingshot hurling her towards an unknown future. It would be three more months before she was due to deliver the child. She had watched her little brother being born by her stoic mother, so she understood from an outside view, but she would be amongst strangers. How would Catholic Sisters treat an unmarried Protestant woman, even as a paying guest? That would be a question soon answered. The Grey Nuns, as they were called, of Notre Dame du Sacre`Coeur, had catered to the poor and ill for the last sixty years, even through the cholera and typhus epidemics. At least she was High Anglican — the nearest to the Catholic faith as any outsiders could be.

Minnie washed-up in the bathroom as best she could on the swaying train. She must look like the wreck of the Hesperus, her mother's favourite reference to a shipwreck.

Back in her seat, Minnie shared the cake with little Michelle. The girl's mother passed her two apples and soon the little one's eyes closed once again. Minnie made herself as comfortable as possible but it was a long time before she slept again, thinking of the day to come.

Dawn was breaking as they arrived in Riviere-du-Loup. The family beside her packed up, the mother turning to Minnie with an outstretched hand. "Merci, Madame. Bon chance," she said nodding at Minnie's roundness, shaking her hand firmly.

Everyone so far had been so kind. It surprised her after so much anger expressed back home. But families always, in her experience as a teacher, had such expectations, whereas strangers did not. She had let down everyone she cared about. Her greatest sin, she realised now, was that whatever happened, it was a relief to be away from the low voices and the eyes shifting before contact. No, at least she was free to pay the price and move on.

The price of course, was giving up her child. Not as painful an option as before if Mary Cobourn's offer of adoption was real. She would have to let the nuns know, but she would remain silent until she was more certain of her situation at the convent.

Very hungry by lunchtime and not certain when she would be able to eat later, Minnie made her way to the dining car. She nodded to the young man who had helped her the day before, who rose to his feet when she passed his table. Finding a single seating beside the window, she

IMAGE 3

was pleased with the thick stew she was served, along with fresh buns and tea. She felt quite worldly. Following beside the vast Saint Lawrence River the train passed little villages covered in a deeper blanket of snow than rural Nova Scotia had been. Montreal would be cold, but it was unlikely she would be allowed anywhere until after the birth. Minnie sighed. The next few months would be a trial, but she had her faith and her self-reliance. That, she prayed, would see her through.

The train slowed as it passed through the industrial area surrounding the entrance to Montreal. Horses pulled every kind of load, ships lined the port entrance and other trains rushed by on nearby tracks. Minnie straightened her hat over her brushed and neatly pinned hair, buttoned her coat and donned her gloves. Placing her small reticule over her arm, she waited by her trunk, hoping someone would help her move it to the platform. The same gallant young man who had been so helpful the day before stood up with a smile and offered to carry it down the steps. There he waved over a porter, then turned to help his mother and father to the platform, glancing back at her with a small nod.

Minnie followed the porter to the snow covered station entrance, clutching the convent address, and feeling very lost and small. Horse-drawn buggies awaited in line, their breath rising in the cold air. When it was her turn, she handed over the address to a wizen driver in a cloth cap. He said something in French Minnie could not catch, it being spoken too quickly.

"Une, trois, huit St.Pierre, Notre Dame du Sacrè Coeur, s'il vous plait, monsieur."

Flustered, she couldn't remember the word for street, let alone numbers, but he nodded then jerked his head toward the carriage door. Minnie gestured to the trunk at her feet.

"Baah," he grunted, getting down as he twisted the reins around the brake. Then noticing her condition, he opened the door, lifted in her trunk and held out a rough hand to help her up the small single step.

"Merci, monsieur."

"Bien," was the only reply.

It was colder inside the jolting carriage than outside, but in no time they turned into a curving driveway in front of an imposing grey stone building that seemed to go on and on. The driver shouted in French to a man coming down the front steps who turned to point further down the lane. Near the back was a smaller annex, although not small compared to any house Minnie had ever entered. Square with more of the same grey stone as the façade, and red brick at the sides, the only relief to the plain design were rounded corners on the roofs edge. "The Montreal Convalescent House" with a repeat below in French, was painted on a small sign outside.

As the driver helped her out, gently placing her trunk in the snow at her feet, he collected coins out of her hand, raised his cap and resumed his seat behind the steaming horses. A plain faced nun dressed in a grey and black habit opened the door. Seeing the trunk sitting on the walkway she turned to speak softly in French to someone inside. Two young women wearing simple headscarves and plain grey dresses came out, smiled at Minnie and picked up the trunk by its handles. The senior nun signalled for Minnie to come in, holding the door open just wide enough for the girls and Minnie to slip through, then closing it with a clang and drawing a bolt sharply into place.

The first thing Minnie noticed was how dark the hallway was and how cold.

"La salle nombre neuf, assez vous," the Sister told the waiting girls.

Turning to Minnie she said in heavily accented English, "I am Sister Marie Trembley, the Sister in charge. We have been in this building since August. Our mission is expanding, thanks be to God and our Mother Elizabeth Bruyere, so we rent out the main building and are fewer here with much less expense. Your accommodations here as a paying guest as we sometimes have, widows and such, will be more comfortable than in our old residence. You must, however, follow the house rules. I will bring you the daily schedule. Your Reverend has sent payment for the three months of your stay, but due to your condition you will not have the freedoms a normal paying guest would have."

Minnie tried not to take offence at the "normal" reference, putting it down to language differences. Following the girls with her trunk, she climbed so many stairs her legs trembled. They made their way higher and higher, up to the fourth floor. Her room was small but really nice. A single bed with several blankets, a mirrored dresser, a wash stand with pitcher and basin, a rocking chair with a small footstool and a hand braided rug made the room look comfortable indeed. It was also warmer with a small water radiator in the corner. This was more than she could have hoped for. A window, facing the curving driveway, was lined with heavy drapes to help with the draft and maintain privacy.

One of the initiates smiled and said in English, "I will bring you some towels and show you where the water closet and baths are, after Sister Trembley explains the schedule."

Her smile disappeared at the tap at the door. Sister Trembley stood back as the two girls bowed their heads and scurried away like grey mice.

"Here you are, Mademoiselle Healy," said the Sister, handing Minnie a piece of paper. "You will be asked to be prompt and not disturb the order and silence of this house. We will answer questions but not engage in chatter. Your clothes will be stored, as well as any perfume or makeup. We live simply here. You will not be permitted to wander the building or indeed go outside, except to the garden, such as it is, at the appointed time. The classes on the sheet are for initiates, not guests as yourself, so please if you need to fill those hours there are services you can do to be as productive as possible during your stay. Any monies you carry or jewelry you wear will be locked in my office and returned on your day of departure. Letters written must not be sealed; they will pass through me before being sent on. Not being Catholic you need not attend chapel but if you wish to you may sit in the back pew by the door. The Sisters and our initiates will speak only when spoken to, so any unnecessary conversation is discouraged."

Another tap at the door, opened to a breathless girl holding a bundle of clothes. Sister Trembley pulled a simple folding screen out of a small closet and said, "Please, change now, and then hand me your purse and jewellery."

Minnie did as she was told, relieved to be out of her coat and dress at last. The new clothes were soft from many washes and had ties that could be loosened as her waist expanded.

Handing over her items she asked, "Would it be possible to bathe, I have travelled for two days and my new clothes are so clean. I also have a small watch I'd like to keep so I won't be late, and my own Bible, if that is acceptable."

The letter from her father and her sister's note were folded in the cover and she did not want to lose them.

"I also have a small cross on a chain, may I still wear it?" "That would be acceptable, oui," the nun said. "There are only two others on this floor so you may not hear us going to chapel or to meals, so remember to keep your watch wound. You are Anglican? We do not take in many Protestant women here, especially now we are so small, but Reverend Moody is much respected and speaks well of your family. You may write to him to let him know you have arrived safely. You will be charged a penny from your funds for postage. Are there any other questions?"

Minnie had a dozen questions but shyly shook her head. Later. She would see how things worked here as the days moved on. She removed her house shoes from her trunk, her under things, a nightie, her hair brush, her toothbrush and powder, her bible and the last of her writing paper and envelopes, all under the silent observation of Sister Trembley. As the good Sister left, one of the young women returned carrying towels.

"Come on, you have time for a warm bath and a rest before supper," she said, grinning. "My name is Bertha." Smiling back, Minnie told the charming girl her name and gratefully followed her down a long hallway. She had to pee again.

IMAGE 4

In the days and then weeks that followed, Minnie adapted to the Sister's schedule. With the changes made so her interaction with the nuns was minimal, she found it not so different from days on the farm. Cleaning up after meals, doing the laundry and ironing replaced going to chapel three times a day or taking classes in French and hygiene. She washed supper dishes while the nuns walked in the snowy garden, and then had her turn before bed after they returned for chapel. It settled her to walk in the bitter air; calming her mind before sleep.

As to the other paying guests, the older widow was religious and joined the nuns in their schedule, never introducing herself to Minnie. In contrast, Bernadette, who was in the room closest to her own, was also in the family way, although closer to her delivery date than Minnie was. She was from Basque in northern France and was married. Her husband, Jean, was first mate on a steamship. They had sailed together to Montreal, but unfortunately he had fallen during a storm and badly broken his leg. He was still in traction in the hospital a month later. Bernadette had moved from a lonely hotel room to the Convalescent House for the remainder of her "laying in wait," as she called it.

Glad to have an acquaintance her age and one in the same condition, it brightened Minnie's day to see her new friend's smile. It was difficult for Bernadette to be quiet but they would meet to speak softly in each other's room or link arms as they walked with ungainly steps around the frozen pathway in the garden. Bernadette's husband, when he was well enough, would find a small house for her and her baby. The streets were too snow bound and busy for him to navigate even when he could use a cane, so for now they were content to be apart, to wait for the birth and a spring thaw.

Five

One evening as Minnie gathered her coat and shawl for her evening stroll, Sister Trembley signaled her to join her in the office. Minnie had sent a letter to Rev. Moody with praise for the Sister's care and expressed her gratitude for his introduction and aid in her behalf. Expecting maybe a letter in return, Minnie smiled at the expressionless face of the elder nun and sat stiffly in front of her desk.

"Mademoiselle, I wish to say your presence here has been most acceptable and your help in the kitchen and laundry room has been a blessing," she said.

Minnie nodded, waiting, suddenly feeling apprehensive.

Sister Trembley continued, "I wanted to make sure you understood our standard procedure with situations such as yours. Have you seen the birthing room? Non? It will be made known to you. It is away from the Sister's rooms, of course, on another floor. A midwife will assist you and a doctor will be called if — and only if — unforeseen difficulties arise."

She looked straight into Minnie's eyes and spoke in a softer tone.

"The child will be removed immediately and you will not see it again. If it is not living or dies shortly after, it cannot be buried in sanctified ground, having not been baptised. Other arrangements will be made."

She made no indication of what those arrangements would be.

Minnie's mouth went dry but she had to ask, "Adoption. What is the procedure for adoption?"

The senior nun sighed. "A protestant child, if it's healthy, will go to the orphanage here in Montreal. We are not an agency; we only assist women here out of Christ's compassion and Mother Mary's love for all mothers. You will have no part in the child's life after its birth and no say in the adoption process. You can imagine how complicated our lives here would be if we tried to satisfy everyone's wishes."

Minnie nodded, imagining strangers coming in to view babies in their cribs and the Sisters doing night feedings. No. Minnie stood.

"I understand. Thank you, Sister Trembley."

She would have to figure out a way to contact Mary Cobourn discretely. But how to do this if all her letters were examined before being posted? The timing was complicated as well. There would be little time after the baby's arrival, and how would they know which child was hers in an orphanage?

Outside, Bernadette looked at her friends pale face in the snowy blue twilight and felt a rush of sympathy, but waited for Minnie to speak. They circled the garden twice as Minnie explained her problem.

"Mais, ma fille, I have a solution," Bernadette said. "When I go to visit Jean in the hospital, I will send your letter to Madame Cobourn, yes? We will ask her to come to Montreal, near your delivery time and wait. When you are in labour they will not notice if I go to the telegraph office — it is beside the hospital where my Jean is. We will tell her to come quickly."

Minnie thought for a moment. No, it would not work. Bernadette would have her baby first. How could she go out carrying a newborn — possibly in the cold night? Maybe she wouldn't even be staying at the House that long; their birthing dates were a month apart. No. There had to be another way.

Awake late into the night, she realised she had to let Mary know what the problem was. If the baby was taken to the orphanage as soon as it was born how would they know which child was hers? Mr. Cobourn only agreed to the adoption because he knew the parentage. If all went normally, the child would arrive in about six weeks. Perhaps they could come and speak to Sister Trembley before the birth, but Minnie was not supposed to have anything to do with the adoption process. She was too tired to think any further.

The next morning while the Sisters were at mass and Minnie and Bernadette set out the breakfast dishes, they tried to find a solution. Bernadette turned to her with a grin.

"I make a plan. We do not tell Sister Trembley this Mary has met you on the train. We pretend Monsieur and Madame Cobourn have met with Jean and me, as if our husbands knew each other in business. We meet for tea, and of course talk about our new child, bien. So it comes out they would adopt but cannot bear going to the orphanage. Oui, so Jean and I tell them we have met this good Protestant woman who is about to have her baby and has to — how you say — give her up? So then the Cobourns come here to speak with Sister Trembley privately, as if they did not already know you from on the train. Bien. Then when the child arrives, the Cobourns are waiting, and the much relieved Sister will send for them right away."

Minnie thought about this all morning. So many things could go wrong and to deceive the nuns after all their kindness was so sinful somehow. Bernadette could not stay long after the birth of her baby. The place was not suitable for a child's presence with its crying and extra laundry. Even her food would have to be carried up four flights of stairs, already a slow climb. What to do? But before Bernadette was too heavy to take a carriage to the hospital to talk to Jean, Minnie had to write a letter for her to post to Mary Cobourn, and Edward. Dear God. How could she receive a reply? She knelt with difficulty beside her bed and prayed.

Bernadette had been wondering the same thing and asked at the post office about whether a mailbox or general delivery would be better. She could pick up the replies and give them to Minnie secretly, as long as it was before her own baby's birth. That afternoon Minnie sat down to carefully compose her letter to Mary. The first hurdle to their plan was getting Bernadette's husband, Jean Seguin, on board. During Bernadette's visit the next afternoon, he was concerned about her travelling even to see him so heavy with their child. When he saw how emotionally involved with Minnie's predicament she had become however, he relented, not wanting to upset her at this delicate time in her life. She promised to always take a covered carriage and not to travel late in her pregnancy.

The post office opened a box in her name so the replies could be received without risk. She placed Minnie's letter in an envelope with a note from her explaining the name and address that replies should bear. There was a postal wicket in the hospital lobby for patients and doctors, so it was easy for her to access. Now they had to wait and see if Mr. and Mrs. Cobourn would agree to the subterfuge. Bernadette's expected delivery date grew closer and Minnie's anxiety grew as well.

Six

Two weeks later, after a huge snow storm had paralyzed Montreal and prevented any trips to visit the hospital, the roads were finally cleared. Bernadette told Sister Trembley she had to check on her husband's health and she really needed to get out for a few things before the birth. One of the young initiates hailed a coach at the main road, saving Bernadette the trip down the snowy lane.

Arriving back from the hospital with rosy cheeks she reported to the waiting Sister that her husband was out of traction and thumping around with a cast and cane. She opened a bundle with a smile showing her tiny shirts and nappies purchased at the hospital commissary.

After a slow climb up the stairs to her room, an impatiently waiting Minnie raised her eyebrows to her friends sparkling eyes. Reaching into the neck of her blouse, Bernadette produced the long awaited letter. Minnie sat on the edge of the bed with her eyes closed for a moment before opening it with a trembling hand.

"Dear Mademoiselle Healy, this reply was a long time coming because we are deeply buried in snow here. Laval is a very small village and we live above it on a hill, so we must wait for the roads to be cleared before going into our store that serves as our post office. It also gave me time to talk to my husband, who was reluctant to accept a child through deception. However, as I told you earlier I have felt in my heart our meeting was not an accident but was touched by the hand of our Merciful Lord.

Edward has come around; knowing perhaps not the details, but that this child was made with love not violence and the community you and your family come from is not unsimilar to our own. My husband says I only think of a child, while he is thinking about what kind of person they will become, and justly so.

Thereby we agree to your plan to go to see Sister Trembley. We shall tell her we have heard through meeting Jean Seguin, a business associate waylaid by a broken leg in hospital, that they, the Sisters, have taken in a healthy Protestant woman (unusual for a Catholic institution and a subject of interest to us) who must give up her child.

This we will proceed to do as soon as we can travel. Edward actually does business in the marine trade — the banking end of things — and does have meetings to attend later in the month of March, in Montreal. We will be staying with friends at the Redmond House and will leave a reply at the hospital post office after our meeting with the good Sister.

Please be well in heart and body, with affection, Mary Cobourn.

P.S. We have a servant girl who is nursing her second child and has agreed to be a wet nurse for your child as well. Providence provides."

For the first time since realising she was with child, Minnie put her head in her hands and wept. Ever practical Bernadette found as many handkerchiefs as she could in her dresser and sat with her arm around her friend. Finally wiping her eyes and blowing her nose, Minnie leaned into Bernadette's soft shoulder.

"I don`t know why you have been so kind to me, when so many would have turned their back, but you are the best friend I've ever had, and I am so grateful for all that you've done. I am in your debt forever."

"Ah, ma belle fille," a smiling Bernadette whispered, "you have carried your burden thinking you are alone. Non. God's love is there for all of us. Have you not felt it since your journey began?" Minnie remembered Rev. Moody, her father's letter, her sister's little cake in her trunk, the porter's tea service, the young man with the glasses, and the young French mother and child. "Yes, I have been accompanied by angels, but you are my favorite angel."

Minnie took a deep breath. She was not a nervous person, but perhaps being so close to her child's birth she was overly emotional. She had been so worried, and it wasn't over yet, but she felt new found hope that things would work out for the best.

"How is Jean? I didn't even ask, but you should rest now and put up your poor swollen ankles."

"Jean is well, healing fast and bored with hospital. We will live in a hotel after the child comes and start looking for a proper house when the streets are clear. I want to keep in touch, so may I have your aunt's address in PEI, yes? Life will go on and things will get better. Now you are right, we must rest."

Minnie helped her friend out of her dress and covered her with blankets; her round belly looked like a snow drift under the covers.

The days slid by turning February snow into March slush with no chance to get to the hospital post office to check for Mary's report on her and Edward's visit with Sister Trembley. Bernadette's water broke after supper hour while she was doing up the dishes and Minnie was mopping the snow melt from the Sister's return from the garden. Bernadette's moans turned to laughter.

"Mon Dieu, He sends a mop to clean up and at a convenient time, so I don't disturb the Sister's schedule!"

Minnie caught one of the initiates in the hallway who ran to fetch the midwife after informing Sister Trembley. With the Sister on one side and Minnie on the other they slowly climbed the stairs to the second floor birthing room. The Sister gathered towels while Minnie helped Bernadette out of her clothes. She was plumping pillows when the midwife arrived in a swirl of cold air.

"Away, away, maintenant, merci!" she said, dismissing everyone.

Minnie spent the night pacing her room, rocking in her chair until her back ached, or lying on her side feeling her own child moving restlessly. Perhaps she (Minnie was very sure it was a she) understood her own time was near.

After a very full bladder awoke her at dawn, surprised she'd slept at all she made her way slowly to the water closet, and then stopped to listen at the top of the stairs. Bertha, the most cheerful of the initiates was climbing up the last steps, her face illuminated with a beaming smile.

"Ach, Bernadette is fine, and has a robust and healthy boy child. Eight hours, tres bien, she did very well for her first child. They sleep now and a message has been sent to her husband. Bien, would you like a bath Mademoiselle?"

Minnie would have liked nothing better, except to visit her friend, which would have to wait. She was getting very good at waiting.

Seven

The next day she was hesitating outside the birthing room door, when a breathless man with a wool sock covering the bottom of a leg cast struggled up the stairs to the second story landing. Minnie introduced herself and reached out her hand. To her surprise he reached into his jacket pocket and placed a letter in her hand, putting his finger to his lips. Smiling, he tapped on the birth room door and entered, closing it softly behind him. Shoving the letter in her pocket, she tried to hurry up the two flights of stairs to her room, but at the top had to stand until a dizzy spell passed.

"Steady, girl, steady," she remembered her father's words.

Closing her bedroom door, she sat in her rocking chair until her heartbeat slowed. Smoothing out the crumpled letter with Mary's now familiar script, Minnie held her breath and read the long-awaited message that meant so much.

"Minnie my dear, we have just returned from a short meeting with your caretaker, Sister Marie Trembley. A humorless but well-meaning and obviously devoted woman, she had been informed by a note from me a few days before, and had no chance to refuse us as I mentioned we were staying in town and would arrive at this time and date. I believe this gave her time to check on our credentials with our well-respected friends at Redmond house. She was assured that we could provide for whatever needs a child could have and that it was wanted by both of us. She understood why the idea of a visit to the orphanage was out of the question, Edward was very firm on that point, and she seemed relieved to not have to send a newborn there. After some tea and a few more polite questions about where we live, she produced forms from when they were in their larger facility and operated a small orphanage and "home for unfortunates," as she put it. We signed the forms, my dear, with trembling hands. It made this so much more real for us, and I know it will relieve your mind to know we are waiting with arms wide open.

We will return home to ready a nursery and be back at the end of the month when you are due — or sooner if the Sister sends us a telegram that the birth came earlier.

May blessings from Mother Mary surround you, my dear. Be at peace, and thank you for your trust. Mary Cobourn."

Bernadette remained another week, staying in the birthing room so she didn't have to climb the stairs. Minnie felt perhaps Sister Trembley was putting some space between the tender family and the unwed mother. It was difficult for her to see the nursing child in his doting mother's arms. It made her realise, for the first time perhaps, how difficult the outcome would be for her. Being on her own this last month would be the most trying.

March weather was always erratic in Montreal. Winds from the north were still frigid, while warmer air brought in by the St. Lawrence River from the Atlantic collided as fog, rain or more snow. It stirred up emotions held tight by citizens confined indoors all winter. Police were kept busy attending to domestic violence, bar fights and errant children; no one understanding why they were so restless.

Minnie's emotions were like the March winds, blowing east then west, and then turning calm after a good cry. She realised she had never been really alone. Rocking in her chair by the window, she watched the leafless branches swaying outside. Trying to compose a letter to her family to ask them for her aunt's address in PEI she felt completely different from the woman who had left three months before. She was focusing on the future now and found her feelings had changed in so many ways. The naïve girl she had been was gone. The reality of her situation brought on by no one but herself, plus the kindness she had been shown by so many, had made her more humble, less critical and more appreciative of how her actions had affected those around her. She came from simple people, dependent for a century on the small community around them. Deeply ashamed at how she had embarrassed her family, she saw her moment of passion had been a childish rebellion against tradition. This time the letter sent to her parents from a contrite and wiser daughter even brought a smile from Sister Trembley as she reviewed and then sealed it with a nod. Minnie would never know her father kept it in the back of his Bible for the rest of his life.

She had started attending afternoon chapel, kneeling at the back on the hard wooden prayer bench. Helping the initiate Bertha with the meal preparations and dishes was the only human contact she had now. Her walks in the garden at twilight were slower, careful not to slip on the still frozen puddles; with the Sisters at evening prayers no one would see her if she fell.

Eight

The first pains struck late in March as she was hanging up her coat in the back hallway. Breathing slowly she made her way to the chapel. She bent with her head on the pew in front of her as the pain swept over her like water over the bow of a ship in a storm. As the Sisters slipped quietly by after the short service, Bertha looked at the sweat slicked face held up to her and signalled another grey clad initiate to help get Minnie to the second floor birthing room.

It was too soon to call for the midwife, so Bertha settled with her Bible and rosary in the rocking chair beside the rubber sheeted bed. Through the long night Minnie really felt she was on a ship, sliding up and down on waves of pain so intense she felt the next would drop her down into a void never to return. Then she would feel a cold cloth on her face and neck and hear Bertha's sweet sing song voice, like a mermaid floating on the waves around her.

By morning Bertha was replaced by a less gentle midwife, who got her up and walking between contractions. Twelve hours of labour and Minnie was tired and not a little scared. Something was not right. By lunch time, the midwife's oils and hot towels had helped but not enough for the child to pass through. Minnie was pushing now, with a piece of leather between her teeth to stifle her screams and to prevent her from breaking her teeth. They called the doctor.

One look at the situation and he growled, "I should have been called hours ago!"

Laudanum drops were given relaxing her enough to allow him to widen her cervix with a scalpel slice; careful not to touch the baby's head now so very close. Using a squirt of lanolin oil he gently eased the little body out, handing it to the midwife to suction and clean. The body remained limp until held upside down over her knee and thumped on the back. A liquid drained out of her mouth followed by a ragged breath that turned her little face red, pulsing with new life.

The doctor raised his eyebrows as the midwife wrapped the baby's navel and started dressing her in the tiny clothes that Bernadette had thoughtfully left.

"Unwed mother, so the child is to be removed immediately," she said in French, glancing at the unconscious woman. "Hold on one moment," the doctor said, raising his hand. "I may need her to nurse the child to expel the afterbirth. It is not coming easily, and that usually works."

This was against instructions but the doctor's orders ruled, so the midwife gently laid the baby against the sedated mother's breast and watched until the child latched on. At least it would have a full tummy before being handed over.

A wail from Minnie a few minutes later with another gush of blood and fluid made the midwife lift the baby away and place her in a bassinette. Turning back to the mother, she gasped. Another little body had slid out into the world! The doctor cut the cord and held the tiny form upside down thumping it until a choking cry broke the tension. He always felt awe at this moment no matter how many deliveries he

IMAGE 5

attended. Trading places, the doctor let the midwife clean up number two and place her at her mother's breast. She was barely conscious but instinctively nestled the tiny head in the crook of her arm while the baby nursed.

The midwife slipped out to see if the new parents had arrived while the doctor attended to Minnie. Because the labour had been so long the Cobourns had had time to receive the Sister's telegram, take the morning train and register into a nearby hotel. Now they were downstairs awaiting word. Hearing muted voices in the office; she knocked and nodded to the anxious faces.

"Oui, all is well," said the mid-wife, "are you ready now?"

Mary Cobourn stood, one hand over her mouth, the other gripping her husband's shoulder.

"Is the mademoiselle alright? This took such a long time! Is the child a girl or boy? Yes, we are ready, our carriage waits outside. I brought this..."

She handed the midwife a fur lined bunting bag. The tired midwife brushed it with her hand and smiled.

"It is a little small for two, but the girls are used to being close together. One moment, please, and yes the mother is fine; very tired and sedated. It is good to do this quickly before she wakes."

As she closed the office door she smiled again as she heard an intake of air and the husband's voice say, "Two?"

Placing the now peacefully sleeping little girls in their soft and warm bunting bag, she glanced at Minnie. She was sleeping again after another dose of laudanum. Separating mothers from their babies was the part of her job she disliked the most, whatever they had done, but obviously the people downstairs would be thoughtful and caring parents. The mother wouldn't know that of course, not even that she'd had twins. Sad, but that was the price of sin and hopefully the beginning of a better life for everyone now.

The best part of that long delivery was placing the children into the arms of the adoptive mother. Mary turned her radiant face to her husband, "Now we are a family, Edward. We have been doubly blessed!" With a laugh she said, "And I won't have to put you through this again!"

Guiding his wife to the door, he leaned over the midwife placing money in her hand whispering, "They are both perfectly healthy, yes?"

"Oui, monsieur, both are healthy in every way." Turning to his wife with a smile now, he said in mock surprise, "Good heavens, you were going to put me through this again?"

The jingle of the horses harness faded down the lane and the house once more descended into silence.

"This was a very difficult delivery, eighteen hours," the midwife said, putting on her coat. "The mother must rest for at least a week with lots of broth and liquids. Please make sure if she has any problems, to call me or the doctor quickly. It drained her physically and emotionally."

The Sister nodded. "I will have Bertha see to her when she wakes. She wants to be a nursing Sister. It is good for her to see how difficult that life can be."

Personally Sister Trembley was grateful for her choice to be a bride of Christ and not have to go through the trials of child birth.

Minnie awoke at twilight, 24 hours after the slow climb to the delivery room. She ached everywhere; her mouth was dry and her brain sluggish. She reached down to touch her empty and very sore belly, the skin that had been stretched tight for so long now slack. Tears came then, running down and wetting the neck of her night gown. Fragments of memory popped up, of the pushy midwife, a male voice, the soft tug of a child at her breast. It was over now.

She hoped Mr. and Mrs. Cobourn had made it here in time. She began to understand for the first time the magnitude of grace she received to have this woman placed in her path, at that moment. How could she have surrendered her child to an orphanage? A day old, how would they have fed and cared for her like a mother would, even an unwed one? How could she live not knowing the details of the adoption? Maybe Bernadette would stay in touch with Mary and pass on how her child is doing. But that wouldn't be fair to anyone. No, she had to put all this behind her and live her own life.

Bertha's smiling face peeked around the doorframe. "Qu'vais tu?" She held up a bedpan. "I warmed it up for you."

Minnie smiled back, her heart filling up with gratitude, and not just for the warm bedpan.

Nine

Ten days later Minnie received an answer to her latest letter to her father. It included money for her ticket to Charlottetown, and enclosed a letter from her aunt Margaret. She sounded so very different from her mother. Margaret was younger and had married a farmer who bought land in fertile Prince Edward Island and raised a family there. She had two daughters, one Minnie's age, one much younger and two sons, who farmed with their father. Cheerful and to the point, her aunt had warmly invited her to join her family and as she quoted "move away from her sorrows." Minnie liked that phrase, and tried not to imagine how her child was faring at the Cobourn's.

Her trunk was returned and Minnie put on her own clothes before deciding to spend a bit of money to buy gifts for her aunt and family. She could not go empty-handed. Montreal's streets were a mess but April had arrived with the smell of spring in the still cool air coming off the harbour. Following Bertha's directions, she made her way to a huge fabric store. She needed some summer clothes and would make some dresses for her aunt's family at the same time, and maybe some shirts for the men. It would give her something to occupy her evenings. Passing a small book store she decided to add two books as well; one suitable for a child and one about the history of the Maritimes.

The next day she said her goodbyes, hugging Bertha tightly and shaking the cool hand of Sister Trembley. The train would take her back to Halifax. Her aunt had suggested travelling with a fisherman friend who owned a trawler bound from Charlottetown, PEI's largest town, for the Halifax harbour in Nova Scotia. This was a better alternative to a long and uncomfortable coach ride to the ferry in Cape Breton that went over to PEI daily. The friend would be in Halifax harbour for several days and his boat would be tied to the dock when her train arrived at the main station nearby. Looking at the price of the tickets that included a sleeper, Minnie decided that she could afford the extra cost since she didn't have to pay for the long coach ride in Nova Scotia, or a place to stay while waiting for the ferry. She would also eat in the dining car. A new life and a new attitude were in order. She may never take another journey so why not enjoy this one before she became a farm girl again?

When she stopped that morning to say goodbye to Bernadette, Jean and baby Louis at their hotel, Bernadette clutched the address Minnie gave her to her large bosom and declared their friendship eternal. Minnie smiled, knowing life may change many things but her affection for her first best friend would remain in her heart forever.

The train ride was fun. Her meals were very good and her little room a calm oasis, rocking her to sleep in comfort this time. On arrival, and leaving her trunk in the Halifax station lockup, she wandered down Barrington Street under the Citadel, to the docks at the harbour's edge. It took an hour of looking and asking for The Grand Dame amongst dozens — if not hundreds — of boats, but the fishing vessels

IMAGE 6

had their own spot at the furthermost dock. It made Minnie hold up her head, she hoped, like a proper lady, while passing several "Ladies of the Hour." Without her family and friends to help her, she could have ended up the same she realised, looking into the face of a girl, barely out of her teens.

With relief, she found the boat at the fisheries dock and the round faced captain Frenchie, who owned her. Warmly shaking her small hand with his rough scarred one, he sent a man back to the station with her trunk ticket. Offering a cup of tea inside the crowded, tool covered wheel house, Frenchie told her they were leaving on the first tide the next morning, early. She could stay at one of the modest but decent bed and breakfast places one street away. He gave her the address of one he preferred and, promising to store her trunk safely, returned to unloading his fish.

Making her way uphill a block from the harbour, Minnie passed several heavily painted women, their gaudy and dirty clothes flapping like flags in the cold sea air. The bed and breakfast in question was pink, inside and out, bedrooms included, but was clean and modest in price. The landlady regarded her with a squint behind tiny glasses and promised to get her up in time for Frenchies departure.

Free to wander for the afternoon, Minnie continued up the hill to the Citadel and the acclaimed view of the harbour. It felt so good to be free, filling her with a hunger for more out of life. Or maybe she was just hungry. Minnie stopped at a small café to lunch on a fish fillet and fried potatoes. Delicious.

Not wanting to return to the bed and breakfast yet, she window shopped down cobblestone streets, stopping at a yarn store to purchase a warm pair of gloves and enough rose coloured wool to make a pair of mitts. Her boots needed new soles but would have to wait.

Too tired to think about going out for supper, she bought a jar of chowder and a biscuit from a merchant on the dock who served the crews that scurried like monkeys over the rails of the nearby ships. Maude Henry, the matron of the bed and breakfast made her tea and heated up her chowder while telling Minnie it was not suitable to go out after dark because a nearby "Madame" operated several brothels, hence the "Ladies of the Night" she had encountered.

"Been there a hundred years; police don't do nuthin," Maude declared. "Shameful, but you know sailors!"

Minnie didn't know any sailors but it seemed to her a harsh arrangement. She had an almost hot bath in a very cold shared bathroom, and crawled under the pink duvet on her narrow bed for an early night. Then she crawled back out and knelt to say her prayers and to thank the Lord for all that had saved her from a much more difficult path.

Ten

Up and dressed quickly before dawn after the landlady's tap on her door, Minnie put a homemade scone Maude offered in her pocket and slipped out into the darkness. The cobblestones were wet and dangerous but the walk to the waiting ship was a short block. A few slumped bodies in doorways took Minnie's glance away from her focus on her careful footsteps. Any accidents that prevented her from reaching her aunt at this point would be disastrous, and for a moment she felt very vulnerable but the good captain hailed her from the deck and came down the gangplank to assist her.

She sat out of the crew's way in the wheelhouse until they had left the harbour behind, and then made her way to the bow to watch the slowly blooming sunrise. This was her last day of total freedom. As the weak April sun warmed her face, a growing sense of more to come overtook her. Was it destiny or a purpose yet unknown or maybe just a giddy relief that her ordeal was over? Squaring her shoulders she faced the horizon, as the distant grey mound of Prince Edward Island rose from the sea in the distance.

It took most of the day for Frenchie to guide his sturdy fishing boat north-east past mainland Nova Scotia, through the Strait of Canso which lay between Cape Breton and the Acadian villages on the Nova Scotia side, and then across the North Umberland Strait to PEI's Murray Harbour. Sharing her scone and sipping some strong coffee, Minnie learned it was much shorter and safer to go this route rather than go around Cape Breton, through the very rough seas of the Cabot Strait. Villages on the north side of PEI had a more difficult route and would often leave their boats in Souris or Georgetown, villages up the east coast from Frenchie's Murray Harbour destination. He told her about the ice boats that used to travel over the North Umberland Strait between the village of Borden-Carlton in PEI and New Brunswick, the shortest route for supplies in the winter.

Shaking his greying curls, Frenchie said "Some got lost or went through the ice and were not found until spring. Now they have a new railway that runs from one tip of the island to the other. This is the train route you will take to your aunt's home in the town of Summerside. It's brought an easier way to move supplies and people across the island, especially in the winter."

"But," he said, shaking his head again, "the early trains sometimes toppled from their narrow tracks because the local government wanted to save money by purchasing steam trains with less width and narrower tracks. The island nearly went bankrupt after two years and was bribed into joining Confederation in 1873, when the government in Ottawa offered the funds to complete the railway."

She would be boarding the train in Murray Bay where one ran six times a day, some for freight, and some for passengers. "I suggest staying over in Charlottetown for the night, as it will be too late to get as far as Summerside, and besides, your aunt lives on a road outside of town."

While Frenchie kept an eye on the tide as they came into the North Umberland Strait, Minnie opened her trunk to check on her funds. She still had several pounds from her father's letter that she opened — it seemed now — so long ago. She didn't want to leave money in her trunk, which would have to be stored in the Charlottetown train station. Another adventure by train!

"Charlottetown," Frenchie told her, looking through his salt splattered windscreen, "is a busy city now, with a new three-storied stone building for the province's government agencies, surrounded by wide streets and gardens. They even have these new-fangled telephones, not that country people would ever see them," he snorted.

Murray Harbour came into view. After tying up at the dock, Frenchie went to the stables to get his horse and rig, giving Minnie time to look around the harbour. There wasn't much to see other than the dock, storage sheds, and a few brightly painted houses perched on the slushy hills surrounding the bay. The mouth of the harbour was guarded by several small islands that must have protected the homes from the worst winter winds. The isolation before the railway must have been daunting.

Placing her trunk and his box of supplies in the back of his horse drawn wagon, Frenchie helped Minnie up into the high seat and pulled himself up beside her. Guiding the horse smartly up the muddy main street past a two-storied general store, a Catholic church and a rough looking working man's saloon, they soon pulled up to the small wooden train station. Helping her down, and gathering her trunk in his arms, Frenchie stopped to check the schedule. "The next train to Charlottetown comes in an hour; it's already four o'clock so you will be there by six. Not too late I hope for you to find accommodation and some supper. You won't be able to let

IMAGE 7

your aunt know your arrival time, so better you hire a transom in the morning after your train arrives in Summerside." He told her to ask for Louis Bertram, he knew her uncle's house well.

He refused any suggestion of payment, so she pressed the book on Maritime History into his hand.

"You're a good girl, Misses. I've known your uncle Jack a long time; it's a good house you'll find there. They will be happy to have you," he said. Looking around he said "You'll be safe here. I'd stay but my wife sees my boat and waits by the window. I'll treasure the book; we've not many in English." Pulling on the brim of his well worn hat, he returned a wave from the ticket master, took his seat in the rig, and slapping the reins, moved up the hill to his home on the cliff.

Sharing a welcomed cup of tea with the station master after buying her ticket to Charlottetown, she asked after a decent rooming establishment near the train station.

"That'd be at Mrs. Hilstrom's, if she's room. Her's is a short walk to the right, outside the station entrance, down on Humber Street. She's got a sign outside. The station has a lock up room, so's you don't got to worry about your things." Checking his pocket watch he nodded as the sound of a steam engine filled the air and shook the wooden floor.

After carrying her trunk inside, then helping her up the steps, he waved to the engineer whose head was visible outside the open engine room window. Minnie settled into her seat, tired but exhilarated. She'd never had so many experiences and things to think about. She felt reassured about the reception she hoped to receive from her aunt's family. She would work hard and try not to be in the way, but she felt so alive!

The light was beginning to fade but the green hills, bright red earth and quaint houses she glimpsed were not unsimilar to the landscape near her valley home in Nova Scotia. It wasn't her home anymore, except in her heart, although even that place seemed estranged.

She needed food soon, she realised. Getting emotional at this point would not do. An hour later she stepped off the train, saw that her luggage was secured and stopped at the tiny window in the main room that served some food and pots of tea. After finishing a bowl of hot chowder, not as good as the one in Halifax, but enough to restore her, she turned right at the station entrance and walked quickly so she did not appear to be an abandoned single woman.

Several drivers for hire with their horses tied to posts in a line, doffed their hats and offered their services.

"I can take you safely to your destination, Misses," one man said softly, cloth cap clutched tightly in his hand.

"For the morning, perhaps, I'm only going a short distance at the moment," she said and smiled at his disappointed face, until he smiled back, doffing his hat in a salute.

She really was getting quite worldly, she thought. Humber Street wasn't far and it was quiet compared to the main thoroughfare. She found Mrs. Hilstrom's Victorian home, with its "Rooms for Rent, Ladies Only" sign. An aproned maid opened the door, looking her up and down, then up and down the street, as though checking for men hidden in the bushes lining the entrance. Yes, they had a room available, and at a reasonable price. Mrs. Hilstrom entered in a swish of tightly corseted silk, looking formidable in her upswept hairstyle and tight lipped scowl. A previously 'worldly and self assured' Minnie felt like a stray cat under her scrutiny. Yes, she would only be one night then on to visit family in Summerside. Yes, she was travelling alone, her trunk already at the station. Yes, she had come from Halifax, and the weather had had been fair. Yes, she had eaten and would like a bath. Yes, she would pay cash now for the bed and breakfast. Please. She swayed, suddenly so tired she almost cancelled the bath, but knew it would help her sleep better and be fresh in the morning. It was going to another very busy day ahead.

After a good night's sleep in a comfortable but rather chilly room, Minnie joined the other guests at the breakfast table with a shy nod at the dower maid. A bowl of hot oatmeal porridge was dropped rather rudely in front of her. A basket of rolls and very good strawberry preserves were within reach, politely passed by a matronly woman seated beside her.

"Coffee or tea is in the cart behind you dear," she whispered, as the maid slipped behind a flapping kitchen doorway without offering any beverages.

No one spoke above a soft murmur, discussing nothing more personal than the train schedules or visits to the government buildings downtown. Minnie had two hours before her train left for Summerside so, her curiosity piqued; she decided to have a quick look at the new and rather grand government buildings and gardens.

Trying to keep her skirts out of the red mud, she walked the few blocks to Queens Square, as it was known. It was indeed impressive. The Legislative Assembly met in the grey, stone three-storied Province House, but its columned frontage and large windows reminded Minnie of her first glimpse of the original Convent House in Montreal. She turned away towards the large gardens. There wasn't much to see at this time of year, but it was obviously very well-tended. When the gardens lead to the wide commercial streets further on she retraced her steps back to the train station to retrieve her trunk in time for the first passenger train to Summerside. She was nearing her journey's end.

Eleven

Accustomed to train travel by now, Minnie got one of the busy porters to get her trunk onto the luggage rack of the wheezing train and found an empty seat by a window. They travelled inland at first and joined another track heading around to the other side of a neck of water that stretched past Charlottetown proper. It passed many buildings of varied industry, then farm houses, and large barns and fields, with black and white cows standing beside puddles of snowmelt. Closer to Summerside she could see the grey waters of North Umberland Strait beating waves against red cliffs. Boats were warned by a wooden red and white lighthouse perched on a narrow spit of land facing the pounding surf. Forests of evergreen trees still crowded the tracks here and there, but much had been cleared for large fields; now lying wet and fallow.

Minnie was surprised to glimpse several bedraggled tents and shacks that had natives sitting on skins outside. None looked up as the train sped by. She knew Mi'kmaq had lived in the Maritimes for centuries, but it always surprised her how desperate they seemed. Maybe she was just ignorant of how they lived, having little contact with those who lived in Nova Scotia. The women sold pretty, sweet water baskets door to door in the summer and were always so shy, never speaking a word.

As Summerside came into view, Minnie's stomach tightened in excitement. An incorporated town since 1877, it now held over two and a half thousand souls. On a lovely, sheltered bay with large beaches and green hills of fertile soil, it had been inaccessible except by boat until the railway had opened up more opportunities for commerce and the trade of farm produce. They passed a mill busy with horse drawn carts and surrounded by some large houses. Wool was the export; it would seem, by the bundles on the platform by the train station.

Minnie straightened her clothes and donned her gloves. It was starting to rain as the porter carried her trunk to the waiting lorries outside. She retrieved her short cloak out of it before turning towards the men and asking in a firm voice if a Mr. Bertram was present. A kind-faced gentleman of uncertain years, and a lip covering mustache of grey, held up his hand.

"At your service, Misses. Jack McLeod's place you're wantin? Sure Misses, I know them well."

He had pulled a canvas up over the transom to keep out the damp and covered his horse with a blanket that he now used to spread over the trunk at her feet.

"Please sir, could I pay you now," she asked, "to prevent my uncle insisting he pay when we arrive?"

Louis Bertram laughed, showing tobacco brown molars. "Your uncle's a Scots; he'd pay me in apples. Thas ok, Murphy," he nodded toward his horse, "he likes them fine."

He took her coins and placed them carefully in his vest pocket before picking up the reins. He didn't speak again but guided his horse out of town and along a wet forested road. They passed a small church with no steeple, just the usual crowd of stone markers. Anglican she saw on a small sign out front built in 1829. It had been so long since she had attended the familiar services, tears caught in her throat. Soon, she hoped, if her aunt and uncle attended.

She had lost track of the day of the week. No matter, she would soon be subject to someone else's decisions again. Minnie sighed. She had enjoyed her three days of freedom. As the driver turned his horse into a grassy lane, a house with a double peaked roof was visible beside a large barn and several outbuildings. Closer, as they followed a wooden rail fence, the house became a faded white with two stories and a veranda roof over the entrance. A woman appeared in a white bib apron, shielding her face with her hand. Minnie's heart was suddenly thudding in her ears. She had arrived.

A New Life

IMAGE 8

Twelve

She could hear her aunt calling to someone. A young boy joined her on the step, and then raced off towards the barn, yelling loudly for his Da.

Aunt Margaret McLeod had a plain but open face as she reached up to help Minnie down from the wagon. Tangling her skirt in the transom's brake, Minnie fell hard into her aunt's arms, nearly knocking them both to the ground. Her blush of embarrassment was hidden by her aunt's warm hug and Margaret's deep, genuine laugh made tears sting Minnie's eyes.

Held at arm's length, her aunt looked into Minnie's face, and shaking her head said, "Oh my dear, I'd know you anywhere. You are the spitting image of your mother. She always was the pretty one."

People seemed to be pouring in from all directions, all sizes, and all talking at once. As Mr. Bertram carried her trunk to the veranda steps, a tall lanky man with dark sideburns came from the barn, wiping his hands on a rag.

"My husband Jack just finished with the milkin'. You catch us as we are, young lady, no fancy manners here," Margaret said.

Her uncle Jack's long face broke into a shy grin. Reaching out his hand to grip hers, his eyes twinkled with a silent message of welcome. The youngest boy, Ronald, or "Racey," as they called him, was the high energy twelve year old. Martin was the oldest son at sixteen, gangly and silent, standing by his father. They were so alike they appeared to be the same person at a different age. Sarah was a freckle faced eight year old with a frizz of hair springing out from braids of strawberry blonde. A gap in her teeth made her grin even sweeter as she took Minnie's hand to lead her inside, out of the damp air. Minnie turned to thank Mr. Bertram, in time to see her uncle loading a box of apples behind Murphy the horse. The driver raised his hat in goodbye and turned the wagon back down the lane.

Her aunt held open the door saying, "My oldest daughter, Amelia, was married this Christmas time. She is Mrs. John McEachron now. They live three farms over. I've missed her and the extra pair of hands. You'll have her bed in the room with Sarah. We have four bedrooms and another extra room that's too cold in winter for humans, but it has an extra bed for summer guests. If you don't mind the chill you can have it now, if you prefer your privacy, or you can wait another month when things warm up, and then it's yours. Lord I'm babbling. I'll go put the kettle on; you must be cold and weary from your travel."

Minnie looked at Sarah's expectant face and said she didn't mind sharing. Martin carried her trunk up the narrow stairs to a room in the back of the house, facing a long open field and the distant blue of some bay.

"Malpeque," he said softly. "French, mostly."

The kitchen where the tea was served was bright with yellow paint and wood trim, a pump sink and a large wood stove. A clean but busy place as most country kitchens were, it smelt of the still warm brown bread served with molasses and dark tea.

Minnie entertained with tales of her journey from Halifax. She didn't mention Montreal and no questions were asked. The boys, as her aunt referred to them, left to finish chores while the light held. Minnie noticed kerosene lanterns. Her father had refused to use them for many years because they were so volatile. Neighbours lost several barns and one farm in the valley had burned along with many animals and one old man, who was sickly and unable to get downstairs in time. She knew how to render fat and make candles from endless dipping and also the easier method of molds, but her mother had insisted on lamps. Sewing by candlelight might be romantic but it made women go blind, and her father could not argue with that.

As she helped her aunt clean up after tea, Minnie assured her she could and wanted to help in any way with sewing, knitting, or cooking. She was fully trained in preserving fruit and vegetables or meat, could milk a cow and hoe a garden. Margaret smiled and said again how glad she was that Minnie had come to them.

Then speaking more seriously and looking intently into her niece's eyes, she said, "So your emotions seem steady and your heart sound, yes?"

"Everyone in Montreal was very kind," Minnie whispered, hoping for no more discussion of the still awkward topic. "I am ready to start a new life."

"Good," said Margaret. "You will find this community a hard working bunch but we have fun. One reason I chose Jack was to get away from our Father's farm. I found that end of the valley in Nova Scotia a little too humourless.

Good people but conservative to the point of being closed up, yes? I understand. You will love the dances here — fiddle playing and lots of building and quilting bees. The old families here had a hard time and things are not easy, but they're getting better. A lot of the back breaking work of setting up the homesteads is done, now it's just the hard work of survival left. That's life everywhere I guess, but if you don't enjoy your home, family and neighbours, it would all be so pointless, yes? Enough. Would you like a rest or shall I show you around? We have twenty milking cows, one bad old bull, a dozen sheep, chickens, one pig and Jenny the horse. We have enough apple trees we can ship some of the best off, but mostly it's our potatoes that bring in the cash to cover expenses. It's a lot of work planting and harvesting but the soil here is agreeable to choice spuds. We will have some for supper."

The women put on their cloaks, but Margaret hesitated looking at Minnie's boots. "Let me go get Amelia's old rubber boots. The farm is always messy but especially this time of year." They fit.

Supper that night, after grace, was filled with a lot of laughter and chatter as steaming bowls of food were passed back and forth. Minnie really liked all of her mother's family who were so alike and yet so different. Things here were discussed, argued, shared and everyone was included.

The house was comfortable, a little worn maybe, but had sturdy furniture, some she was told came from Jack's family in Scotland. Some standing cupboards were hand carved with leaves and flowers, and a rocker that seemed to be everyone's had a pressed oak leaf back. Large jugs and platters that were made for a large family, had painted scenes that added colour to the wooden corner cupboard. Jack had raised a larger section of the house and attached it rather handily to the original homestead. "Abandoned," he said, "when the French moved enmass over to Malpeque Bay to avoid being expelled by the English. Past nonsense," he growled. "They were good neighbours; still are."

He had known Frenchie as a child playmate and had been glad of news that he was doing well. While Margaret got the younger children ready for bed, Jack told her a bit about the local politics. He seemed to not know or care it wasn't discussed with women who could not vote or own property yet. So Minnie listened while he spoke about absentee landlords asking for rent from people who had crossed an ocean to avoid just that. "Huge tracks of land were "owned," said Jack, "by wealthy men from overseas who sent agents to collect rents once a year. They would remove anyone who couldn't pay. Then there were tensions between Catholics and Protestants, even locally sometimes if someone wanted to marry outside their religion. Schools, such as they were, were divided; the rich from the ordinary, in supplies, teachers available and subjects taught. Working class children worked alongside their parents and often schools were too far away to travel to in bad weather, so education was sporadic at best. Things are better now, but we still have problems."

"You've been a teacher, Lass?"

Her bent head and small nod stopped further questions from him, but after a pause as he tapped tobacco into his pipe bowl, he said, "Well then, you can help the little ones with their readin' and such, yes?"

She looked up into his kind face and smiled. She was going to like it here!

IMAGE 9

Thirteen

Minnie passed the rest of a wet, cold April getting to know the rhythm of life on the McLeod farm. Slipping easily into her role of helpmate to Margaret, she enjoyed the chaos of breakfast, the chores around the house and the peaceful quiet after lunch when she worked on her sewing.

Margaret was thrilled with the fabric brought all the way from Montreal. Patterns littered the dining room table. They would enlarge them for the growing children, or alter them for more modern styles Minnie and Margaret saw in the women's section of the newspaper delivered to the mailbox at the end of the lane.

By May, a softness returned to the breeze from offshore, and buds poked out of tree branches and bushes. Working on a summer dress for herself, Minnie realised her body had changed as well. Good food, exercise, and of course childbirth had given her a sleeker but fuller body, with larger breasts and wider hips. As she thought of Jack, Margaret and the children, she felt so grateful to her second family, as they had become. There was security in the affection they had for each other despite spats or differences of opinion. Laughter was heard often through the doorway to Minnie's sewing room, as the formal dining room had become known. She heard Sarah telling the new doll Minnie had made for her out of scraps of material, "You have to be good because you've been made by the best cousin, ever."

Jack and the boys had been preparing the tools and machinery for the planting of this year's potatoes. Small hills of musty, fungi-smelling seed potatoes were shoveled out of the root cellar, their alien eyes already sprouted like tangled white arms. The earth, red as rust, was still wet as Jack plowed neat furrows with a team of borrowed grey percherons. Martin followed with the harrow, carefully pushing the soil into long strips; the tractor's tires making pathways in between. When the sun warmed the soil enough, individual mounds were formed by hand and a seed potato was dug down deep in the center. It was dirty, back-breaking work, with the women pitching in when they could get away from housework and animal care.

Too much rain would rot everything, and unseasonably cold temperatures caused the potatoes to go dormant, waiting, growing small and green. This year the gods blessed the fields with all the right weather. Minnie was preparing supper as she looked up to see a tired mud covered family come back into view. Jack reached out and took Margaret's hand in his, lighting her face with love. Minnie wondered if she would ever feel like that again. Her heart was so closed to her past brief passion; could she ever open herself up to someone else? If she revealed her shame to them, would she be rejected? There was lots of time ahead before that needed to be considered, but still her heart felt squeezed in a vice with just the thought.

One of the happiest summers of her life lay ahead. As the potato plants grew and the apple blossoms filled the air with their intoxicating scent, the spring lambs were born and the strawberries ripened in the sun. Amelia, the married daughter, came for lunch with her proud husband to announce she was in the family way. Small glasses of sherry were raised in celebration; even the children had a taste.

Minnie couldn't help feeling a twinge of jealousy and maybe regret. She hid it behind a smile and raised her glass to meet Amelia's gaze. She liked Amelia's straightforward manner, which was so much like Margaret's. She wasn't pretty, but handsome with thick curly brown hair and her father's soft brown eyes. Her husband was a homely man, no way around it, and a bit course. But with no formal education, thought Minnie, how else could he be?

She decided to renew her efforts to get the children to read and regretted briefly giving the history book to Frenchie. Maybe a trip to town to find a book shop or library, if one existed, was in order.

When the heat arrived in late June, a trip was organised, but not to town, to the beach in Malpeque Bay. Swimming costumes were unearthed from trunks and a picnic of vast proportions was prepared. All piled into the back of a cleaned-up wagon behind Jenny the horse and off they went, singing French songs to practise the language spoken there.

"Malpeque," said Jack, over his shoulder, "is the French spelling of the Mi'kmaq word for "big water." The natives had been the first settlers thousands of years before the French had arrived in 1534. After the fall of Fort Louisburg in Nova Scotia, the British arrived in Prince Edward Island and ordered the expulsion of all French citizens. Due to the lateness in the year and its sheltered bay deemed too shallow for large ships used in the deportation, Malpeque remained in French hands."

The huge beds of oysters, supplied to the restaurants in Charlottetown and Summerside, kept the small community of Malpeque busy. Margaret didn't like the slimy shellfish but Jack stopped to buy some from a cloth-capped fisherman he knew who would have been offended if he didn't. They would buy some fish on the way back, to keep it fresh. The beach of fine sand on the north-west side of the bay was large and quite breezy, but, finally with a day to just play, the children ran squealing into the waves as all children do.

Minnie walked quite a long way, picking up shells and enjoying the respite from work as well. The whisper of the waves enveloped her and she loved staring at the endless blue of the ocean. Lunch was cold cuts, fresh bread and strawberry shortcake for desert. Jack tried to get her to eat an oyster and laughed at her expression until he lay down on the sand, as she held the creature in her mouth, unable to swallow. Margaret passed her a napkin in sympathy so Minnie could spit it out uneaten.

"An acquired taste," said Jack still grinning and wiping his eyes.

Back in the village of battered but brightly painted houses, Jack bought some fresh and dried cod, and some seaweed called dulse. Minnie tried it and quite liked its salty taste and chewy texture.

Wiping the sand out from between her toes before climbing into bed that night, she breathed deeply in and out, feeling strong and at peace.

Summer days galloped along with the washing and carding of wool added to Minnie's chores. Not having sheep on her father's farm in Nova Scotia, she was experienced in the preparation and weaving of flax but not wool. Spinning flax was a nerve wracking job but wool, soft and pliable, was a pleasure to her. Under Margaret's gentle instruction the spinning threads became smooth and even. The weaving would be done later in the slow days of winter. Margaret used marigolds for yellow, onion skins for orange and nettles for green, dyeing only small batches in the overly warm kitchen.

"Just enough for trim on mitts and sweaters," Margaret said, her face wet from the steaming vat she stirred. "It's the old way to dye but holds so well when rinsed in salt and vinegar." Any old apples went into a barrel and were made into vinegar. The softest belly wool from young sheep was washed repeatedly to be knitted into long underwear.

"And now I'll be knitting a lot of baby clothes for our first grandchild, God willing," Margaret said, smiling.

Fourteen

The trip to town was to coincide with July 1st celebrations held in Summerside; it was mainly to see neighbours and get supplies. Confederation had really been forced on the people of Prince Edward Island, so they were content to be left alone, similar to most immigrants' experience with the Crown.

The ladies put on their new summer dresses and lighter straw bonnets. The boys struggled to button new shirts and to flatten down sun-bleached hair. Jenny the horse got her tail braided, her hooves polished and her coat curried to a shine. The tandem was pulled from the barn and cleaned of chicken droppings before blankets were spread to keep clothes clean. Little Sarah had been making fabric decorations for weeks and her brothers helped tie garlands around the wagon bed and pin rosettes onto Jenny's bridle.

"You did a fine job with the decorations, young Sarah." said Jack.

Her gap-toothed smile was a mile wide at her father's rare praise.

"I am going to make pretty dresses like Minnie when I grow up," Sarah said, tracing the lace trim on her sleeve. "I can almost reach the treadles on the sewing machine now, so next winter Minnie's going to show me how to make big things."

Margaret reached over to squeeze Minnie's hand. "You've done well with her. She misses having other girls around to play with and sometimes I know she feels left behind. Today we should meet neighbours with daughters close to her age. There's talk of a new teacher coming this autumn; we'll see. We raised a new school building five years ago and then old Mr. Hennessey died, so no new teacher all this time. You've been a great help getting our children to read and such; not an easy task."

Passing the church, Minnie saw an elderly man coming out and shutting the door sharply behind him.

"Old Thunder and Guts hisself," murmured Jack.

"Now dear, don't be so irreverent. He just takes his job seriously," said Margaret.

Turning to Minnie she spoke softly. "The Reverent Mulcair has turned many people away with his overly zealous attitude. Farming people like to get together, but we were all so miserable after his sermons and surprise home visits, only a few still attend services on a regular basis. Jack refuses to go back."

"I'm not getting dressed up to take everyone out in bad weather to get yelled at by a man who has never done a hard day's work in his life!" Jack said, frowning, his back stiff in anger.

"Now Jack, we are going for a day of fun, don't get all upset before we get there," Margaret said. She rested her hand on his arm and he turned his face to her with that lopsided smile he had just for her.

"You're right, as usual, Mrs. McLeod," he said, pushing his shoulder against hers and relaxing into her air of calm.

The sun shone down on the sweet smelling forest and the meadows full of wild flowers that they passed, as their tandem joined others near the town of Summerside. Martin and Racey jumped out to join other boys they knew, with Margaret calling after them to meet in the food tent later. Jack doffed his hat at neighbours waving at them as the crowd grew along the dusty road.

Minnie got a few hard stares; it was the first look at the cousin that had joined the McLeod family.

"I told them you were coming to help out after Amelia left us," said Margaret. As always, it seemed, she was so aware of Minnie's feelings.

"Thank you," whispered Minnie.

"Well, it's true, isn't it? You are like another daughter to me, and I've grown very fond of you," Margaret whispered back.

Another chunk of ice in the back of Minnie's heart that she didn't know was still there melted. She took a deep breath as they entered the town square.

Jack helped them out of the wagon, and then went to stable Jenny out of the sun before joining the other farm owners at the beer tent.

"We have the morning free," said Margaret, taking Sarah's hand. "So, what would you like to do first?"

"Go watch the games!" shouted Sarah, whirling in a circle.

All the younger children played simple contests like running with an egg on a spoon, the three legged race or the jumping run, done with a burlap bag pulled up to their waists. Prizes were given and much coveted by the winners.

Minnie spotted a bookstore on the main street and agreed to meet at the food tent in an hour. She had brought some funds and hoped to find some books to further instruct the children and maybe something for herself. A little sun-blinded as she entered, with the door bell tinkling overhead, she waited a moment for her vision to adjust, before stepping forward. An ancient man appeared behind a worn wooden counter, peering beneath a pair of wire spectacles perched on his forehead. He nodded and waved his hand as if to introduce her to an audience.

"No one else here, Lass, so the place is yours. I'm in the back having my tea, so when I can be of help just ask. I'm Samuel McKnight." He raised his eyebrows, waiting, nearly displacing his glasses.

"My name is Minnie Healy. My aunt and uncle are the McLeods. I live with them now."

"You're from Nova Scotia, Lass? I heard some such from customers, and you've the accent. Was there something in particular you're looking for, or would you like to look around undisturbed? I didn't expect many in today with all the festivities. I've seen it all many times and would rather go later when it's cool."

"I'll look for some books for my young cousins' reading practice, and maybe a novel for myself, if I may," replied Minnie, a little dismayed at being the subject of local conversation. But that was normal in a small community, although Summerside seemed a large town to her.

"Glad to make your acquaintance Miss. Let me know when you are ready." With another wave he disappeared behind a dark curtain beyond which Minnie could hear a kettle whistling.

Most of the books were worn and stained but well organised. There wasn't much for children but she found a few titles she recognised from her own childhood. Martin was the most difficult of the children to interest in reading, being almost a man himself, but she found a well-worn copy of Moby Dick. It would hold his interest and probably Racey's later. A newish copy of "Ladies Home Journal" was a welcome find, as well as a book about travelling in Western Canada. She noticed more women authors were publishing under their own names, or perhaps a pseud-onym? She found a knitting pattern magazine for Margaret in an open desk top, and then finally a small book about the adventures of Annie Oakley that took her fancy.

She called out for Mr. McKnight, and he appeared with a smile and complimented her on her choices. As he wrapped her purchases in brown paper, the door bell signalled another customer. Turning, Minnie could only make out a dark silhouette outlined against the bright sun-shine outside. Taking her package with a light shake of Mr. Knight's hand she turned towards the door, coming face to face with the young man from the train ride to Montreal; the light shining off his spectacles.

Moving forward he blinked, just as sun-blinded as she had been, and nearly stepped on her toes.

"Ah, Peter, our new teacher, yes your order has arrived. Let me go get it," said Mr. McKnight disappearing once again behind the curtain.

Minnie tried to escape around the young man, who was blocking the doorway.

"Oh, I'm so sorry!" he said, and stood aside, holding his hat while squinting at her.

"My fault, excuse me," whispered Minnie, sliding by him and out the door before any more conversation reminded him where he'd previously seen her. She had obviously been with child when they'd met six months before, and that would follow her to her new life, if he made any comments, especially in the company of Mr. McKnight.

The new teacher, he'd said. She wondered if his school would be the one close to Jack's farm, or in another district, as she hurried to the food tent. The pleasure of her purchases was lost as she thought; the past always catches up somehow.

Finding the others in the food tent with plates piled high with scalloped potatoes and spring lamb or tuna steaks, Minnie noticed a scowling Martin seated beside his father.

"Jack found him chatting up one of the O'Donnell girls," Margaret whispered. "Prettiest one is Marie, his favorite but they are as Catholic as the Pope in Rome, so no future there. It's best stopped now."

Minnie knew from bitter experience how that just drove lovers closer. Racey, on the other hand, was so excited by the pen knife he'd won in the footrace, he talked and ate at the same time. A glare from his father slowed his chatter down, but his eyes still shone with delight at beating the other boys and receiving the best prize. Sarah had won a small embroidery set in the spoon and egg race. Minnie promised to help her with it.

After lunch they roamed the square, looking at tables of cheeses, used household items, piles of handmade, braided rugs, harness tack and polish, soaps and tinctures, and a beautiful exhibit of wood carvings.

IMAGE 10

Minnie moved beside Martin as he picked up a small ship in a bottle. Talking more to himself than her, he mumbled, "I'm off to sea in two seasons, you wait. Racey can take over my place helping Da by then. I'll make my own way, then I'll come back for Marie. We'll be of age in two years, and no one can tell us what to do."

Realising he'd just revealed his plan, he turned to her and pleaded quietly, "Please don't say nothin', I mean anything." He swallowed, "A man's got to be his own self sometime."

He looked down and scuffed at the ground, then glanced up at Minnie. She nodded. She understood, and besides, many things could change future plans, as she well knew.

They sat on their blankets and watched the fiddle competition, the square dancers and then the Highland dance finale. Coming back from the food tent with sandwiches for supper, Margaret pointed out a very attractive girl of sixteen or so who led the other dancers.

"Marie O'Donnell," she murmured with a sidelong glance at her entranced older son, who stood up applauding as the dancers took their bow.

The smile Marie sent him let Minnie know Martin's affections were reciprocated and not so easily dismissed. Martin disappeared for a few minutes, coming back with a bag of fudge for everyone. He handed his father the bag with a smile.

"This a peace offering, lad? Well thanks be to you," Jack said holding the sweet, his favorite, before eating it with his eyes closed.

Calm restored, they chatted to neighbours waiting beside them for the fireworks to begin at dusk. Minnie looked nervously around for the young man with the spectacles, seeing him only once, alone on the edge of the crowd.

Fifteen

The rest of July and August were days filled with harvesting and preparing nature's bounty. Minnie spent a lot of time in the kitchen garden with Sarah, weeding and putting up the produce not eaten right away. It took a lot of food to feed a family of three growing children and three tired, hungry adults. As the apples ripened, some types coming to maturity earlier than others, Minnie helped in the orchard. Apple bags slung across their shoulders, it was heavy work, climbing up and down the specially shaped ladders, and then gently emptying the bags into wooden boxes on the horse wagon.

Jenny the horse kept the clover that was growing between the trees mowed down until she grew drowsy and refused to move, her belly full and her head warm from the sun overhead. Lunch for humans was taken with their backs against the trees; the youngsters blowing on grass blades or running from the honey bees buzzing over the fruit. Jack didn't hire extra hands until he needed them later in the season when the potatoes went to market.

Minnie lay in the clover, as drowsy as Jenny, listening to the chatter and laughter around her. What a contrast to her father's nearly silent days of harvest; the hired men expected to work not talk. It wasn't fair to compare personalities; she loved her father, but she felt so happy here. She felt she was beloved, just as she was part of a unit that worked well because everyone knew they were needed. She wondered how couples just starting out, like Amelia and her husband managed. When she asked, Jack assured her with a smile, "John comes from a large family and relatives always help out. The McEachron's farm is smaller than ours and they depend on dairy cows and the cheese they produce rather than potatoes as a cash crop."

"We trade produce at the end of the season; I've no patience to make cheese," Jack said, waking up Jenny with a smack on her dusty rump.

Margaret stood up, brushing off her skirt and adjusting the pins in her hair.

"I'll be glad when this is over and we go to the harvest dance," she said. "Everyone who can still walk goes to the new school with trays of food and drink, and to dance to the fiddle. It's our reward for making it through another harvest time."

Minnie's ears prickled at the mention of the school. She was going to have to meet the new school master properly at some point. Perhaps she could discreetly discourage any reference to her past. She rehearsed several conversations in her head until she felt certain she could mention a loss, and leave it at that.

Everyone was so tired by evening that not a lot of activity was possible before eyes closed. But as the harvest party neared, Sarah added rosettes to the summer bonnets they would wear, while Margaret and Minnie recut older dresses into more fashionable styles found in "Ladies Home Journal." Jack tested his batch of apple jack and declared it a "good year." Cakes were baked the day before in the cool of the morning because the wood stove oven was easier to control with small bits of wood added carefully. The morning of the party cakes were iced and topped with fresh raspberries and cherries, then carefully placed inside wooden apple boxes in the root cellar until it was time to go.

Margaret braided Minnie's hair and pinned it up in neat circles held by a lovely silver comb.

"This is from Jack's mother, gone long ago on the voyage coming over; his Da gave it to me at our wedding. He's gone now — fishing in winter through a hole in the ice too late in the season," said Margaret. "Jack said he and his brothers nearly starved in the early days here. The French took them in, that's how he knows the man that brought you over from Halifax. Frenchie grew up in Malpeque Bay but he makes a better living fishing from Murray Harbour, and he hated oysters."

Minnie touched the comb as she looked in the hallway mirror. "It's lovely, Margaret, thank you, I'll take good care of it and return it tonight."

She looked so different with sun bronzed skin and rosy cheeks, that maybe the new teacher wouldn't recognise her.

The cakes and the cider jug arrived at the school door in their wooden boxes undamaged from the jolting wagon. Folks poured in from all directions and Minnie's head swam trying to remember all the names as she was introduced. The ladies living closest to the school had turned it into a flower filled room. It had the little desks pushed together to carry extra plates, long tables set out for food and drinks, and the benches were arranged along two sides for seating. The band such as it was, took over the teachers' little raised platform as a stage and were tuning up as everyone headed for the heavily laden food table.

With plates perched on their laps, the women sat on one side of the room like colourful birds on a wire, while the men doffed their jackets, placing them on their bench and stood up, holding their plates in their hands.

Then there was that always awkward moment when the band starts up and someone has to be the first to dance. Jack grinned at Margaret as she rose from her seat, blushing like a maid half her age. Others quickly joined them in a set that was sort of like a square dance mixed with traditional steps Minnie had never seen before. Taking her empty plate back to the food table she felt a presence beside her. Looking up she gazed into the same gentle face she'd met on the train.

"Hello, we meet again. I'm sorry I don't know your name. I'm Peter Harrison, the new school master."

It was spoken accompanied by an outstretched hand Minnie could not refuse. He squeezed her gloved hand, waiting a little longer than necessary to release it, as Minnie tried to remember her rehearsed lines.

"I live with the McLeod family, my aunt and uncle. My name is Minnie Healy," she stammered.

"Did we cross paths at the bookstore in Summerside?" he asked. "I couldn't see properly when I first walked in but I thought I saw you later with your family at the July 1st celebrations."

He was trying to put her at ease but this just made her blush more deeply. She had to say something before he told anything to anyone about their first meeting. She nodded.

"I never thanked you for being so kind to me on the train. It was a difficult time for me. Having suffered a loss later that I am trying to leave behind, I hope those days are never part of a discussion, here or anywhere."

Minnie swallowed and saw something pass over his face as he came to some realisation.

"Yes, of course, our past is no one's business here," he said. "I also am relieved to be living a more independent life. I understand." He smiled. "I hope we can be friends as we're both new to the community. It is really wonderful to see a lively event after so much hard work. Do you dance?"

She and Martin had been practising in the barn, and were both very inexperienced and nervous. They spent more time laughing than rehearsing, but Minnie realised her standing in the community would rise if she took to the floor on the arm of the new teacher. So, off they went to a head spinning start of a reel, ending up breathless and smiling to the applause from those seated on the benches. Several other young men approached to sweep her away until, hot and giddy, Minnie slipped outside.

The men had lit lanterns and hung them in the hallway, as the sun sank behind the trees. The doorway and area around it was filled with tobacco smoke as they gathered to talk and pass the cider jug around.

Minnie walked down the lane to stop and pat Jenny's nose.

"Ah, Miss Minnie, it's good to see your face again!" A voice she would recognise anywhere came from the shadows of the tree-lined lane. She whirled around with her hands over her mouth to prevent a shout that would bring attention from the men nearby.

"Stephen! What are doing here?"

"What kind of greeting is that for an old friend?"

His reply told her he'd been into the whiskey even before his breath reached her nose. He picked her up and was about to dance her around but ended up in a lurch sideways when she pushed his arms away. This caught Jack's eye, who was standing by the door with his friends.

"Go away Stephen," she managed through gritted teeth. "I have nothing to say to you, except you nearly ruined my life. I've started over here and I don't want to see you ever again." Her eyes filled with tears, her happiness gone.

Jack's gruff voice was beside her. "Anything amiss, Lass?" Turning to the blond young man, who swaying and still grinning in front of him, he said, "I think this conversation should be held in the sober light of day. We want no trouble here, so best you're on your way, sir."

Jack's friends moved quietly to stand beside him and, although Stephen's smile never left his face, he turned, glanced briefly at Minnie, and then continued unsteadily down the lane and into the gathering darkness.

Minnie wanted to sink into the earth and disappear as well but turned to her uncle's questioning look, trying to find words to explain.

"He is someone who used to work on my father's farm in the Valley during harvest time," she said. "Thank you, Uncle. I'm sorry to spoil your evening." The last words were directed towards the others who'd gathered.

"No problem, Lass, not the first or the worst extra entertainment we've had at these events, eh lads?"

Everyone smiled and drifted away, lighting cigarettes and pipes and recounting old stories. Jack offered his arm as they walked back up the lane. His body stiffened as they saw Martin and Marie come from the shadows, holding hands.

"It's time for us to hit the road home," he called to the startled lad. "Go get Jenny ready while I get the others. Minnie can go help gather up the cake tins and such; no argument Martin."

Marie gave the now scowling young man a nod, and ran up the steps into the music and laughter.

"I'm not going now Da," Martin said defiantly.

"Yes, you are. Your cousin has had an upset and the young ones are tired out. Sorry son." His voice was gentler now, "This isn't about you."

Martin looked into Minnie's scarlet face, nodded and turned to get Jenny harnessed. Jack led Minnie back inside, turning from her to find Margaret and the children. She found the cake pans and her bonnet and shawl on a bench nearby. People came over to say goodbye and how nice it was to meet her, and Minnie mumbled replies. A sharp look from Margaret as she took the cake pans from her, told her Jack had said something to get them away a bit earlier than expected.

"I'm sorry Aunt," she said.

They piled into the wagon with the children protesting that they weren't tired yet. They were sound asleep by the time they arrived home, so Jack carried Racey to his bed; Martin carried Sarah, and Margaret stirred up the embers in the stove to put the kettle on for tea.

"So, this was more than a casual farm hand's rough approach? My girl, it's apparently thoroughly upset you. Do you want to talk about it?"

Minnie sat in the rocker, her hands clutched in her lap.

"His name is Stephen Connor and he is — was — the father of my child. He doesn't know about that part; he left before I knew, although it wouldn't have made any difference because my father would never have accepted him."

"Stephen is a casual labourer because he prefers never settling down or taking on any responsibilities. It was as much my fault as his; my sin for which I paid by losing my baby. A kind couple adopted her; I'm sure it was — is — a girl."

Her voice trailed off as Jack called "Goodnight!" Then Minnie told Margaret the story of her days in Montreal.

"I've been so blessed by God's kindness. I can't forget that. I love being here with you and your family; I hope you still want me to stay."

Tears came then, with Margaret handing her a hankie and letting the tears fall. Finally, she got up and brought a hairbrush, undid Minnie's braids, hesitating once, and then started brushing her hair.

"I always find this calming. Drink your tea, girl. You'll always be welcome here. Always."

Margaret had hesitated because the precious silver comb was missing from Minnie's hair. She would not mention it, as it risked further upsetting her niece. She'd think it was just part of her undoing her braids and Jack would never notice. It was probably lost during the meeting with this Stephen. It must have been rougher than she'd been told. Trouble on the hoof, that one. Her niece was well rid of him, hard as it must have been.

Margaret sighed. She knew Martin was the next heartache.

The next two days were quiet ones, everyone doing ordinary chores only because Jack had declared they needed a "wee rest up."

Two things happened though that helped Minnie regain her good spirits. The first occurred while she was hoeing weeds in the kitchen garden. Stephen walked up out of the woods, cleaned up and very sober. Minnie's heart pounded but she closed the garden gate quietly behind her and followed him to sit on a stump by the creek. They watched the water flow by as she calmly told him of her pregnancy and trip to Montreal. His apology for her troubles was sincere and accepted. At her insistence he promised never to come to the area near Summerside again.

"I'm sorry too, my girl, for embarrassing you last night. I wasn't thinking, as usual," he said. "You've a good family here and I'll not bother you again."

Minnie nodded, then stood on trembling legs and walked back to the garden as he disappeared into the trees. After lunch she, Margaret and Sarah sat on the veranda, reading. Minnie was enjoying reading her Annie Oakley book. She was such a brave and daring young woman, although how much of her exploits were true was debatable. The same age as Minnie, Little Miss Sure Shot had travelled with Buffalo Bill's Wild West Show and reportedly shot a cigarette out of the mouth of Germany's Kaiser Wilhelm.

At the sound of a horse and buggy coming smartly up the drive, Margaret stood, smoothing her hair.

"It's our new teacher, Peter something. Come to ask us about sending the two younger ones, I expect. Sarah go get your Da from the tack shed and a chunk of ice from the icehouse. I'll make some iced tea with fresh mint."

IMAGE 11

Mr. Harrison — Peter, as he insisted — looked about as he and Minnie waited for the others, then he reached into his pocket. Holding out a clean handkerchief, he pulled from its folds a silver comb.

"I found this outside when we cleaned up the school. I remembered it in your hair when we were dancing. Very pretty and I suspect too valuable to lose."

"Oh Peter, thank you! Margaret hasn't said anything but I'm sure she's noticed it gone. It's hers from Jack's family and a treasured heirloom. She will be so glad it's returned. What a woman not to chastise me for losing it. Thank you again," she said smiling up into those now familiar gentle brown eyes.

Sixteen

Their courtship was a slow movement toward an uncertain future. It really began when the weather turned too cold for Racey and Sarah to ride Jenny to the school house and leave the mare tethered outside. They walked there and back for two weeks until Racey got a heavy chest cold running around outside at recess without his coat on. With Margaret attending to him and preparing meals for everyone, and Martin with Jack taking produce to sell in Summerside, it fell to Minnie to take Sarah to school in the morning and pick her up midafternoon. She and Peter discussed lessons and how much homework or discipline was appropriate. He seemed to really need to talk to someone about what items should be taught at what level.

Renting the small cabin in which the previous teacher had allowed comfort to take second place to his drinking, it was neither warm nor big enough to swing a cat in, according to Margaret. So, Peter was often invited to share a meal with the McLeod family on the weekends. Margaret would smile watching Minnie and Peter; their two heads moving close over some text. Even Martin would join in discussions around the table about his copy of Moby Dick, which he was slowly reading.

By the time Racey's cough had subsided enough to walk back to school it was near Christmas. Peter missed seeing Minnie coming up the path to the school door and, although he was expected to take the two-week Christmas break and go see his parents in Halifax, he found he didn't want to go. However, on receiving a long letter from his mother, hinting at her bad health, he was too dutiful a son to disappoint her. His mother would be curious about his life and any acquaintances he had made in his first placement as a graduate teacher. She wanted him posted nearby in the Halifax area, but he had to go where he was offered work and truthfully, he wanted some distance from his mother's rather overbearing opinions about his future. His father had chosen silence over debate with her long ago.

Christmas at the McLeod household was a busy but easy time. They baked puddings and cookies, and Sarah hung evergreen boughs on every available space. Martin and Jack found a lovely fir tree and placed it on its stand in the parlour. Racey snared two rabbits for rabbit pie, a favourite. Gifts were handmade, created in secret with furtive rustlings and late night projects, hidden away in trunks before being placed under the tree on Christmas Eve. Everyone except Jack, who stayed behind to tend the fire, went to church.

"Finally," thought Minnie, as she tucked blankets around everyone in the sleigh; Jenny's breath showing white in the crisp air. Snow had started mid-December making a fairyland out of the laneway and the surrounding evergreen forest.

The church was full; neighbours nodded and smiled, whispering news before Rev. Mulcair's voice announced the start of the service. For once his sermon was quite short and spoke of the love God has for His children in bringing his Son into the world as a source of salvation to those who believed in Him. A small choir of locals wore lovely robes and sang just a little bit off-key.

Shaking everyone's hand after the service, Rev. Mulcair paused when introduced to Minnie, to ask about her briefly and request an interview for Sunday school classes, if it was something she would like to do. Guessing a letter of reference would be necessary from her past minister; she murmured something vague and withdrew rather quickly. The Reverend advised Margaret to encourage her husband to attend more often and so he received another noncommittal answer. He turned away with a sour face.

"Really!" said Margaret as Martin helped her into the sleigh, "he can't let people just enjoy being there when they can come. No one likes to be told what to do, especially by someone who isn't there to help outside of that little building, a place we made with our own hands."

"Most Ministers are very involved with the community they live in; I wonder what has made him so bitter?" said Minnie. "He has never married?"

Martin snorted, "What woman would want him? No one is pious enough is my guess."

Minnie, thinking of Peter under his mother's control for so long, wondered if Rev. Mulcair had a critical mother who closed his heart to everyone but God. She wondered also if Peter would discuss their relationship; reminding his mother of their brief contact at the Montreal train station. Actually she had been seen before that in the train dining car as she passed by their table, her belly leading the way. It was only ten or eleven months before but it seemed so long ago now. She wouldn't dwell on it and be miserable on Christmas day.

Peter came back a few days early, having told his parents he needed to prepare lessons and write his report to the Department of Education. He had indeed talked to his parents of meeting Minnie again, in the most neutral of terms, but his mother picked up on the unspoken friendship he and Minnie had developed. Her harsh attitude about "that woman" had been very difficult to ignore. His father, on the other hand surprised him on the ride to the carriage that would take him back to Prince Edward Island's ferry. Mr. Harrison senior had asked about Minnie's personality and hearing the joy in his son's voice, laid a hand on his shoulder and said, "Never mention this to your mother, but you were born seven months after our wedding. Many people marry under similar circumstances, and not all choices are for the best. I think your lady has made a difficult choice in the past, but for the better reason. To marry for love, as well as compatibility, is the ideal. It's what I wish for you."

"Thank you, Papa. That means a lot to me," Peter said. "I have no means or home to share with a wife yet and it will take some years before this is possible. I'll go very slowly and be very sure of my choice, but it will be my choice."

"Well said, my son, I'm proud of you."

Peter smiled and embraced his father, gathered his bags, and turned to board the waiting carriage.

Seventeen

It was three years before another posting came, this time to Charlottetown where he had to board at a house approved by the headmaster. The school was a large one with the lady teachers and female students' entrance on one side, and the men teachers and male students on the other. The pay was better, but still not enough to support a wife, so he and Minnie had a romance by mail.

They found it was the perfect venue to express their inner most feelings about many topics. Both cautious people they enjoyed the opportunity to share personal ideals and were delighted by how much they were alike in their beliefs. Minnie had never had a male friend who communicated so easily with her most intimate thoughts. Friendship slowly blossomed into a very deep affection shared by both, scaring Minnie and delighting her with every letter.

Martin had indeed gone to sea when he turned eighteen, so now Racey was helping Jack with the farm work. Minnie did as much as possible, as the days and months drifted by.

Three years later in July, 1886, a trip by train to Charlottetown with Margaret and Sarah, included meeting Peter for tea. Looking even more handsome and mature he led them to a lovely hotel dining room for a formal English tea service. Later, after a slow walk in the now flowering gardens by the parliament buildings, with Margaret and Sarah trailing discreetly behind, Peter and Minnie confirmed their feelings were growing for each other, despite the distance.

"Soon," he said. "I've requested a posting near Halifax that will include my own house and I want us married before we leave Prince Edward Island, so all your second family can be there."

Then he kissed her and placed a small box in her hand. The ring had a tiny stone, but it sparkled and it was hers. At the age of twenty-two she had started feeling like an old spinster; now the future held a new promise.

After saying goodbye, and watching Peter stride off happily, the ladies went shopping for fabric and gloves for Minnie's wedding costume. Another winter and then another spring passed by before the new posting was confirmed. Peter arrived at the McLeod farm in June, after final student exams, with his own horse and buggy and lots of plans.

Their wedding was celebrated in the little church with a new and more cheerful pastor. Fourteen-year old Sarah was the bridesmaid and Jack was the father elected to give her away. Her own father was old now and arthritic, but sent a generous banknote. Her mother remained silent but her sister Mildred, now married and a mother, mailed her a beautiful travel suit. It fit perfectly; they had always been the same size.

Peter's parents would give them a reception when they reached Halifax. Minnie's only sadness was in leaving Margaret, Jack and the children, but Margaret reassured her Amelia was nearby to help, and Sarah was a big girl now. They would wait for Minnie's letters, and hold her in their hearts.

After a honeymoon in Summerside, with days spent wandering the harbour and nights in a seaside hotel, Minnie finally felt complete. Peter was a kind and careful man; intelligent and curious. He was a comfort and she knew a friend for life.

Their first night alone started with a wonderful dinner in the hotel dining room, overlooking the bay. Minnie was nervous until Peter took her hand and led her, not upstairs but to the rose garden outside and a bench in the centre gazebo. The air was sweetly scented, and with a full moon overhead, the garden was as if lit from within.

Wrapping his arms around her, he leaned his forehead against hers and said, "I've wanted to tell you that you are most precious to me just exactly the way you are. I could wish for none other to spend my life with and," he hesitated, drawing a breath, exhaled, and then, breathing into her hair, murmured "I'm so very glad I don't have a quivering virgin in my arms."

Minnie looked up startled, then seeing his grin, burst out laughing. Wiping tears from her eyes she looked into his smiling face and kissed him deeply. Taking his hand in hers she led him to their room, closing the door quietly. Undressing slowly while Peter took off his jacket and lit the lanterns, Minnie felt darkness leave her heart, replaced by a warm softness that she could now recognise as love. She was cared for by this wonderful man and would build a good life with him. They found their bodies fit as easily as their hearts, and after their long courtship, passion was unleashed, finding a home in each other's arms.

Eighteen

She enjoyed the steam ferry ride, aboard the Princess of Wales to Nova Scotia, and even the carriage trip through the Nova Scotia countryside, but dreaded her first meeting with her mother-in-law. Peter's father had evidently had words with his wife about her attitude, that he considered it unchristian and beneath her, and so the first meeting with Minnie was cool but polite.

"Give her time, dear wife of mine," whispered Peter at the reception in Halifax, where twenty guests greeted the new couple.

Relieved that was behind her, Minnie set about making the little clapboard house they had been given by the school board, into a home. Her own home; the very thought made her smile at shopkeepers as she chose fabrics and small accessories. The house had come furnished with aging furniture, threadbare rugs and chipped kitchenware, but was on a tree-lined street in the Richmond area, not far from Peter's school.

Her happiness in the years that followed was marred by three miscarriages, and the death of her father. Peter, surrounded by children all day, was not concerned about being childless at home, but about Minnie's feelings of guilt. She blamed her inability to produce a living child on the difficult delivery in her past. Peter decided to help fulfill her

IMAGE 12

maternal instincts by bringing home boys from the school who were unable to go home for holidays or because of illness. As the years passed, their home provided loving care for dozens who often returned after graduation to visit their "second home," as it became known.

Minnie went back for her father's funeral; staying with her sister Mildred, who was taking care of their now senile mother, in the old homestead. It was difficult to see the changes in the farmhouse where she had grown up and she was relieved to return to her own life in Halifax. Being a teacher's wife had its own social obligations with dinners held for other staff and the constant fundraising.

It was nearing the new century of the 1900s and Halifax was growing quickly. The deep harbour brought prosperity and new immigrants from Europe. Most moved on to other provinces, but many stayed and filled the schools with non-English speaking children. Minnie started a reading program in her living room that was very popular with the younger newcomers. Peter would come home to the sound of children's voices happily repeating phrases that they had stammered over in school. A gentler approach in a non-threatening environment helped the shyest child to enjoy learning. He was proud of his wife and encouraged her efforts.

The years sped by. In 1914, on her fiftieth birthday, Peter booked a dinner in their favorite restaurant, surprising and delighting her by ushering her old friend Bernadette to their table. She was in Halifax to see her youngest son graduate from medical school and had conspired with Peter to make her visit a surprise. She and Minnie had always stayed in touch by letter, but it was so good to be enfolded in that warm embrace again. She stayed for several days, chatting non-stop as they shopped, cooked and entertained the children at lesson time, in English and French. Bernadette had six children, was round and rosy and full of laughter, and still a perfect match for the more serious Minnie.

"Ah ma fille, it is so good to see you settled with your good husband. I sometimes wish for my family in Basque, still we have our own homes now, as it should be, yes? I worry about the political unrest in France and Germany and I get letters from my family that are hinting at more troubles to come. I'm glad we are safe here in this country."

Minnie recalled Bernadette's comment a few months later when war was declared, and even Canada was involved as part of the Commonwealth.

"Common destruction, more like it," was Peter's comment, as many of the young men he had taught came to the door in their uniforms to say goodbye.

"At least we are safe here," murmured Minnie, putting an arm around his waist and leaning into his shoulder.

Nineteen

Because so many young men were leaving, Peter was made principal of the new Richmond school on Broome Street that opened in 1910. He was very proud of the new facilities and was at his desk before 8 AM. Classes started at 9 AM when the teachers and children arrived.

Ships were flooding into the Halifax harbour, deep and safe; it had become a central hub for them before crossing the Atlantic to Europe. With numerous rumours of enemy submarines waiting off shore, they waited there in turn to load and unload at the busy docks.

On December 6, 1917, two of those ships were to change Minnie's life and the lives of thousands of others, forever. The Norwegian ship The Imo heading to Belgium with supplies left the harbour on the wrong side, crowding and then colliding with a French cargo ship, The Mont Blanc. The Mont Blanc did not have her red flag hoisted, so no one except her crew knew it was filled with munitions.

With the outbreak of fire on the deck igniting barrels of fuel, all of The Mont Blanc crew abandoned ship, allowing it to drift for twenty precious minutes toward the city's piers. People came out or crowded at windows to watch the fire, not knowing what lay below the ship's deck. At 9:05 AM, the largest explosion the world had ever known, leveled

IMAGE 13

or damaged every building in a six mile radius. The ship's anchor was blown four miles away.

Nowhere was hit harder than Richmond. It was obliterated in seconds; the rubble in flames. At first, survivors thought they were under attack by the Germans, but word of mouth told that it had been a ship collision, one of them a munitions ship, revealing it as the source of the destruction.

Those people on the ground were either never found or buried under the debris. Entire city blocks were reduced to piles of broken lumber, much of it in flames from ruptured gas lines. A blizzard arriving in the terrible aftermath froze many still trapped beneath what was left.

Minnie had watched Peter leave earlier that morning, raising his hat to her as she watched from their parlour window. She planned to go visit her ailing mother-in law. They had made their peace over the years and the now widowed and lonely senior Mrs. Harrison welcomed her visits. She lived on Robie Street, in a two-story red brick house, tucked away behind Citadel Hill.

Minnie noticed the smoke in the harbour as she knocked on the front door, waiting for the housekeeper to let her in. She was just removing her gloves when suddenly she was flying through the front room, surrounded by shining lights. Waking up dazed amongst the broken glass and splintered wood, she wondered why no one had closed the door. A cold draught whistled through the open gap; no door there. It was not actually missing; it covered the body of the housekeeper nearby, her neck bent at a strange angle. Mrs. Harrison senior, never one to be seen in her morning wrap, had been looking out the window at the smoke as she waited for the housekeeper to help her finish dressing. Minnie found her crumpled and lifeless, a large piece of glass severing her throat.

Looking out the pane-less window Minnie did not understand what she was seeing. Every building was damaged or simply not there. She should find Peter and help him with the children. Walking quickly, she cut through the parade grounds, ignoring the other survivors and the destruction around her. No street signs remained and the further she walked the worse the devastation became.

The school was no longer there; just the foundation amongst the tangle of debris. Unable to find anyone who could respond to her questions, she ran toward her house. Surely Peter would have gone there looking for her. The corner lot where their house had been was empty, except for some twisted pipes and an upside down bathtub.

Twenty

Minnie searched through makeshift hospitals filled with screaming patients and walked past rows of dead bodies in military barracks and government building basements, but she never found a trace of Peter or any of the school staff. She slept fitfully in the housekeeper's bedroom in Mrs. Harrison's house, after the bodies had been removed by exhausted firemen.

Getting up at first light to search again and again, she finally fainted in a hospital morgue. The Red Cross matron who asked her for a relative's contact address sent a telegram to Minnie's sister Mildred, who had been frantic for news. Mildred sent her husband Alfred to escort Minnie back to the Annapolis Valley. The trains of course could not run into Halifax proper, so Alfred took his new automobile, packed with blankets and food, knowing it would be a long cold journey of sixty miles on snowy roads.

It took many cold hours and two flat tires to get there but the most difficult part was navigating the destruction before reaching the damaged house on Robie Street. Snow had blown into the front room through the still broken front door and missing window panes. Alfred found Minnie wrapped in a quilt, sitting in a rocking chair in the back bedroom. He was afraid of startling her when he spoke, his face hidden in the gloom. "Minnie, my wife, your sister, sent me to fetch you, you can't stay here. It's too cold. We can sort things out later." He was stammering, he knew but her staring reddened eyes unnerved him. She was in shock, of course, but in a worse condition than he had expected from a woman who had always been so efficient and in control.

He managed to find enough dry wood in a back shed to start a fire in the kitchen stove, heating water for tea and unpacking the food basket. He realised Minnie had reached the end of her strength physically and emotionally, so he spoke to her softly and treated her gently. Finally warm and full of tea and soup, Minnie slipped under the covers of the housekeeper's daybed and slept. Alfred put the automobile in the shed covering it with a canvas tarp so the radiator wouldn't freeze, before dragging a mattress from upstairs to the kitchen where he slept by the stove, waking twice to stoke the fire as the cold wind whistled through the broken house.

The trip back to the valley was a blur for them both, Alfred peering through the windshield at the road covered in blowing snow, using gas from cans in the back so they wouldn't have to stop; Minnie, bundled in blankets, stared sightless out the window.

THE TRANSITION

Twenty-one

Back on the farm, a worried Mildred had shoveled an area at the bottom of their driveway to park the Studebaker when it arrived. She had been watching out the window as their neighbour had plowed their road hoping to see Alfred's auto coming on this, the third day since his departure. Finally seeing it come into view, she grabbed her coat and boots and waded through the snow to break a path from the door to the end of the drive.

Looking at the drawn faces as she helped Minnie out, she wrapped her arm around her sister's waist to guide her home. An exhausted Alfred followed with the blankets and empty food basket to the house, which was warm and smelled of soup bubbling on the stove. Alfred kissed his wife, then shook his head. No questions yet. Mildred had been nursing her and Minnie's mother since the death of their father, now she had another to care for, but her children were grown and gone and it was a large house. She showed Minnie to the room she'd had as a child, helping her undress and climb beneath the quilts, a warming bottle at the bottom of the bed.

In the days and weeks that followed, Minnie moved around like a shadow, jumping at the sound of a door slamming or the clatter of the cover on the stove wood box. Her sleep was broken by nightmares, repeating her search through bloodied hospital corridors in her mind, leaving her exhausted amongst twisted sheets in the morning light. Mildred gave her simple tasks like sweeping the floors, holding skeins of wool to unwind, or kneading bread, and watched over her sister as she slowly made her way back from her heartbreak.

Strangely, it was their mother who was also lost in her own memories that brought Minnie back to the world of the living. She started taking her mother's food tray to her and patiently feeding her with a spoon; their roles were now reversed from Minnie's childhood. One day Minnie was brushing her mother's hair and started humming a song her mother sang to make her sit still as a child when getting her hair brushed and braided. Startled out of her dreaming, her mother turned to look at her asking who she was in the same sharp voice of her past.

"It's Minnie, Mother, come to visit."

"Minnie's gone away," her mother muttered.

"I went away Mama, but I'm back for a while. Would you like to know what happened to me while I was away?"

Getting no reaction, she told her anyway, all of it. Every day she would take up the hairbrush and tell her more. Mildred, on hearing her voice, opened the door a crack so she could hear as well. And so, little by little, as spring arrived and the snow melted, Minnie told of her life up to when she and Peter were in their home and welcoming the children to their extra lessons in their living room. There she stopped.

Her mother reached up to pat her hand, the first gesture since the onset of dementia and the first touch from her since Minnie had confessed her pregnancy, over forty years before. Laying down the hairbrush carefully, Minnie slid to the floor and laid her head in her mother's lap. Mildred peaked in to see her mother gently stroking Minnie's hair; then smiling, she quietly closed the door.

IMAGE 14

Twenty-two

By summer Minnie could walk amongst the apple blossoms in the orchard, remembering the laughter amid the hard work at her aunt's farm in Prince Edward Island. She wrote short notes to them and Bernadette, letting them know where she was. She told them only the briefest details. Bernadette's reply told of losing her son, the doctor, in the explosion. She said she understood Minnie's grief, as did so many who had lost loved ones that dreadful day.

Minnie helped with the garden and found she could sleep peacefully after some hard work and fresh air. Their mother slipped away to her final rest that autumn and was buried beside her husband in the old churchyard. Many neighbours attended the funeral, nodding at Minnie who turned her face away before anyone could make any comments. She really didn't care who remembered what anymore, anyway.

By the next spring she was restless and felt she had imposed on her sister long enough, but where would she go and what could she do now? The answer came first as a surprise envelope in the mail from the Society of Teaching Members of Nova Scotia. They had rebuilt and offered a small pension to injured teachers or their widows. It was gratefully accepted.

The second surprise came through Alfred's lawyer who had finally released the will from the Harrison's estate. As

IMAGE 15

Minnie was the only family member surviving, she was given the house on Robie Street and an inheritance, if the bank records could be sorted; they were a mess after the bank's destruction.

She got the lawyer to sell the house quickly, since all of Halifax was rebuilding and needed housing. With the funds secured she decided to move to a nearby town on the New Minas Basin. When Mildred and Alfred drove her there, she found a small yellow house for sale on a tree-lined street.

After the purchase was complete, she and Mildred went through the family farmhouse choosing furnishings and linens for Minnie's new home. Each item seemed to bring back memories and stories of family events, bringing them both to laughter at what had been such a serious attitude that had pervaded their upbringing. The next afternoon, in front of Minnie's house while Alfred unloaded the car, Mildred put her arm around Minnie's waist.

"What will you do here? You are too young to spend your life alone," she said.

Minnie looked into the tiny parlour and said, "I'm going to open a reading room and library for children. I miss my books and the sound of children's laughter. I will read them stories after regular school ends."

And so Minnie became a little old lady, much loved for her story time reading to local children on their way home from school.

After her death, she was buried in a graveyard overlooking the red earth of the New Minas Basin and is remembered fondly by three generations of "her" children to this day.

ACKNOWLEDGEMENTS

This little book could never have come to fruition without help from many sources. The library staff on Quadra Island started a writer's night that got me reading my first stories. To Barb, Lisa, Tracy and Mathew for the initial computer assistance, thanks for the gentle beginning. Tell Well Publishing is a young business who assists self-publishers and guides them to completion, without whom this story would never have seen the light of day. My computer guru Julie McInnis, who cheerfully formatted all the bits into what I had only imagined, my gratitude is endless and forever. The amazing artist who kindly allowed me to use her beautiful image for the cover, Katherine Stone; it will forever remain the Minnie in my mind and now others can appreciate the talented lady you are. The many museums who provided the archival images to give a peak into another time, as listed in my Appendix, with many thanks to the people hidden behind the scenes, who helped make the story realistic. And lastly, to Minnie Healy herself, a real person whose fictional life story was whispered in my ear, I hope I have done justice to you as a woman whose real story will remain a mystery, but your name now will be remembered by all who read this tale.

APPENDIX

Appendix

The photographs included in this book are not necessarily specific to the characters and locations here; they are representative of their historical era and are credited below to their archival sources.

Cover Photo
The Shadow of Her Hand II, Artist Katherine Stone

Photo of the Author
JUDITH TAIT by Paul Ryan

Page opposite to Chapter 1 – Image 1
The Anglican Church of St. John, Port Williams, N.S.

Page 4 – Image 2
CPR Imperial Limited 1890, Notman & Son, McCord Museum view 3261

Page 18 – Image 3
Sherbrook St., Montreal 1867, William Notman, McCord Museum view 2446.0

Page 24 – Image 4
Woman hanging washing, 1900, Charles Howard Millar, McCord Museum view mp-1974.133.185

Page 42 – Image 5
Mr. & Mrs. Breakley, Montreal 1867, William Notman, McCord Museum view 128993.1

Page 48 – Image 6
Consolidated Engine no.403, McCord Museum view 2149

JUDITH TAIT

About the Author

Born in one of the Planter houses built in 1777, in the Annapolis Valley, and a graduate of the Nova Scotia College of Art and Design, wherever Judith lives she is still a Maritimer.

Investigating her ancestors led to the fictional life of a real person, Minnie Healy, born in 1864 outside the village of Port Williams in Kings Co., Nova Scotia. No other details of her life were recorded.

This is Judith's first novel.

CPSIA information can be obtained
at www.ICGtesting.com
Printed in the USA
LVHW04s0340090818
586296LV00002B/2/P